House Calls In The Hills

Memoirs of a Country Doctor

by

Jay Banks, M.D.

Mountain State Press
Charleston, West Virginia
1996

International Standard Book Number: 0-941092-35-6

Library of Congress Catalog Card Number: 96-078488

First Edition

Mountain State Press
c/o The University of Charleston
2300 MacCorkle Avenue, SE
Charleston, WV 25304

Printed in the United States of America

Cover Design and Illustrations by Steve Gray

This is a Mountain State Press book produced in affiliation
with The University of Charleston. Mountain State Press is
solely responsible for editorial decisions.

Banks, James W., 1921
House calls in the hills : memoirs of a country doctor/by Jay Banks.
1st edition
1. Banks, James W., 1921 2. Physicians-West Virginia-Biography.
ISBN 0-941092-35-6   LC 96-078488

From inability to let well alone;
From too much zeal for the new
    and contempt for the old;
From putting knowledge before wisdom,
    science before art,
    cleverness before common sense;
From treatment of patients as cases; and
From making the cure of the disease more
    grievous than the endurance of the same;
Good Lord deliver us.

Sir Jonathan Hutchinson (1828-1913)

Contents

THE RISE AND FALL OF KNOWLEDGE

There are times in a man's life when he knows everything. For a doctor, one of those times is the day that he graduates from Medical School. The ultimate pinnacle of his level of knowledge, however, is the day he begins practice in his very own office. From that day, it is downhill all the way.

I stood in the Reception Room and looked about. Reception Room was what I intended it to be called. It never reached that stage. "Waiting Room" is what patients had called such a room forever, or at least since physicians had offices. The room in question, in my office, remained a "Waiting Room" and served its purpose very well.

I was beginning my practice in the village of Beaver, in southern West Virginia. The house that was to serve as my office was a vestige of the lumber camp that had developed around a now extinct planing mill, built by the Ritter Lumber Company shortly after the turn of the century.

I was taking over the practice of a physician who had left to take a residency in Ear, Nose, and Throat, or Otorhinolaryngology for those who have reached the sophistication of calling a Waiting Room a Reception Room. The house was of board and batten construction, five rooms and a bath, and a front porch that stood uncomfortably close to the highway. The outside of the house was unpainted, but the boards had weathered to a pleasing, dark brown patina.

My predecessor had left furniture for the office, consisting of some tubular steel chairs with plastic covered seats, a desk, some instrument tables and cabinets, and a couple of examination tables, one of which was equipped for gynecological exams.

In those days, physicians in the rural areas dispensed a lot of medicines from their offices. Writing a prescription meant that the patient, or somebody, had to drive to town to a pharmacy to have it filled. Also, store hours were a rigid 9:00 to 5:00, and many patients couldn't get into town to have a prescription filled. For that reason it was necessary to have a fairly large inventory of various drugs, and in the rural doctor's office there was one room designated as the Drug Room. In the case of my new office, there was such a room with some rough shelves for the medications that my predecessor had dispensed, which included aspirin in five different colors. With the advances in pharmacology today, it would be almost impossible to dispense medications from your office. It is also considered unethical, and possibly illegal.

There was one room which was empty. I had visions of it being a Consultation Room where I could sit down at a desk, twirl my stethoscope and look wisely at a grateful patient, or family thereof, and deliver the good/bad news. I did put a couch, a table, and a bookcase in the room, and used it a couple of times to have drug salesmen tell me about their products. (Drug salesmen have now become Pharmaceutical Representatives, at least the kind of which I am speaking, and are of mixed gender.)

That's as far as I got with the Consultation Room project. At the beginning I had no concept that walking from one room to another took time. When the Waiting Room is full, and the telephone is ringing about house calls and how soon can you get there, time becomes a sacred commodity that is not wasted on walking to and from a Consultation Room because it looks nice and sounds professional.

The house was heated by open gas stoves, which in summer worked great on a cool morning. In winter I would find that heat was a precious element that could be attained only by firing up the stoves to a point just short of conflagration.

The best thing that the doctor left me was Bessie Greer, his office nurse. Actually she had kept the office straight, perhaps kept some records, and served as a chaperone for women patients with obstetrical or gynecological problems. In time she became quite adept at taking blood pressures, giving injections, doing urinalysis, and other things that made my practice easier and quicker. She also kept the books and filled out insurance forms, most of which were for the Department of Welfare. Most helpful of all was the fact that she had grown up in Beaver and knew practically everybody, their family history, who was related to whom, and where they lived.

I got her a desk, a typewriter, a file cabinet, an office log in which to post the appointments of patients, and an account book, and she was in business as a nurse-receptionist. The idea of appointments went the same direction as the Reception Room and the Consultation Room, and the office log merely kept a record of who walked into the office for professional services. Nevertheless, it was an exciting two or three days getting set up for what I envisioned as the area's answer to Mayo Clinic. I mean I was ready to stamp out disease!

There was no problem in developing a practice. The doctor had left word that a new man was coming. Also, I was not exactly a stranger to the region, having grown up in the nearby town of Raleigh. The fact that my father had been practicing in the area for fifty years, and had probably delivered about half of the residents of the Shady Spring district under the age of fifty, made my name familiar.

Sadly, however, I was beginning my career in August of a summer that was experiencing one of the worst known epidemics of poliomyelitis, or infantile paralysis as it was commonly called. Any child with fever, or any complaint at all, was immediately suspected by the parents of having polio. Unfortunately, many of them did.

My telephone had just been connected. In fact the man was just leaving when I got my first call. It was Mrs. Bennett. She wanted me to stop at her house that afternoon. I knew the name. She had been the Principal at the Elementary School in Raleigh, the year I was in the second grade. We spoke her name in a whisper. When I finished the eighth grade we were still speaking of her in a whisper, and she had been gone for six years.

I walked up the front steps of her house and she met me at the door. She was dressed in a light, summer frock, accented with a pearl necklace. Her gray hair was freshly waved and had a slight bluish tint that complemented her dress. Wire framed glasses gave her a formidable countenance. I had the urge to whisper when I introduced myself.

She invited me in and took her seat on a divan. I stood there, expectantly, waiting for her to voice some complaint, or direct me to the room of a patient.

"Turn around," she ordered, in the same tone that she had used when she used to say, "Go to the blackboard." I turned, feeling her eyes boring

4

through me in the process. "I guess you are all right, but you are never going to be the man your Daddy is," was her final judgment. Then she asked me to have a seat while she served iced tea and cookies.

∞2∞

THE SUBJECT OF FEES

I had only been in Beaver a day or so when I was called to Blue Jay, a defunct sawmill village. The mill had ceased operation in my early years, and I remembered well the whine of the saw and the huffing of the dinky engine that hauled logs from the woods.

The people who lived in Blue Jay had mostly been born there, or nearby. Most had been families that had, in some way or another, been associated with the lumbering operation.

On this particular evening I was called to see Mrs. Cox. Most everybody called her Granny Cox, and to a lot of them she was! Her husband was Henry Cox, or Grandpa Cox, or Preacher Cox. Some called him Brother Cox. He was an old lumber mill hand, timber cutter, a preacher, and storekeeper. He and Mrs. Cox totaled about 180 years of life, and for over two-thirds of their respective lives, they had been together.

Several daughters were present, a couple of granddaughters, and some great, or perhaps great-great grandchildren were playing in the yard. Mr. Cox sat in a rocking chair in the bedroom, rocking slowly, his massive hands folded across his broad abdomen. Mrs. Cox was propped up slightly in the bed, frail, wrinkled, and breathing heavily. Though it was a warm evening she had the bed clothes tightly held over her body. Over the head of the bed hung a photograph of a middle-aged man standing beside a coffin that was suitably propped up at an angle to show the body of a woman, I assume his wife. The photograph was hand tinted. It was an unsettling scene, but one that I would see often, not only on my frequent visits to Mrs. Cox, but in other houses as well.

Taking a medical history wasn't easy. Her soft voice was often drowned out by the booming voice of her husband, or contradicted by the opinions of one of the daughters. Piecing things together suggested that her problem was most likely her heart.

Examination was another matter. She had on at least two night gowns, both tightly buttoned to the neck, and she was very reluctant to have them undone in my attempts to listen to her heart and lungs. The bedclothes that she held closely about her were a formidable barrier to palpation of the abdomen, or to check for edema of the lower extremities.

I decided that she most likely was in chronic congestive heart failure, and as it turned out, she had been taking digitoxin, a digitalis derivative, for her heart and had run out of her medication several weeks ago. They had waited "for the new doctor" to come to replenish her medicine. Subsequent refills would be accomplished by another house call, as was usually the case in the very elderly.

When I was finished and had given all the instructions for her care, and had said when I would return to see her again, Mr. Cox pulled out a purse, the type with a catch that is opened by twisting it between two fingers, and can be closed with a resounding snap.

"What do I owe you?" he asked, pulling some bills from the worn purse. Before I could answer, he continued, "That other doctor always charged five dollars. I'm starting you out at four for a while to see how it works out." He handed me the money and

7

snapped his purse shut with a finality that assured me that the subject of the fee was closed to debate.

A gentle shower had settled the dust on the path out to my car, and the odor of wet grass on a summer evening leaves an indescribable feeling of peace in your body. That, coupled with the frailty and the softness of the voice of Grandma Cox, which I soon began to call her, made the evening worthwhile.

I never progressed to a higher fee while Mr. Cox lived, and surprisingly enough, his frail little wife survived him by several years. She cut my fee to fifty cents.

After Mr. Cox died she moved into a smaller room, moving also the tinted photograph of the man standing beside the open coffin of his wife. It continued to hang disconcertingly over the head of her bed.

Examination never became any easier, because of the number of gowns that she wore. Also, as time progressed, her little body became even smaller until she scarcely made a lump under the cover.

When I would complete my visit and start to leave, Grandma Cox would always fumble inside her gowns and pull out a cloth bag that was tied about her neck. She would take out a fifty cent piece and hand it to me.

"I want to make sure you are paid," she would say. I would thank her and walk out of the room and place the coin on a table beside the front door. Somehow, her daughter would get the coin back in the little bag before my next visit.

☙3☙

FARLEY'S CREEK REVISITED

Raleigh County, east of Beckley, was very rural. The next doctor past my office was in Hinton by one road, or in Princeton by another. Some of the doctors in Beckley were still making house calls out in the country, but for the most part they stayed in town. A lot of them were trying to get away from house calls altogether.

I had been in practice only a few days when I returned to the office from lunch to find Ed Kincaid and another man sitting on the porch. Ed lived in the house next to my office and he had more or less assumed the role of my ambassador. Ed was in his late seventies and a typical Appalachian mountaineer with the characteristic twang to his voice, and the traces of Elizabethan expression to his speech. The man with him was Charles Kincaid, his cousin, a younger, mirror image of Ed.

"Charles lives over in Richmond District," Ed explained, "and his wife has taken bad with the fever, and I allowed as how you would be glad to go out there with him to see her." It was a beautiful day, the office was empty, and I figured I could take an hour or so and run out there. I hadn't been out there for years and years to go fishing on Farley's Creek, and I had no memory of the distance, or of the road on which we would travel. Also, in that span of time, I had forgotten my vow that I would never go to Farley's Creek again.

Bessie asked, "Shall I close up at the regular time?" I assured her I would be back by then. Bessie didn't say a word, but her eyebrows raised slightly.

In weeks to come, perhaps even from that very moment, I would recognize the expression as one of doubt.

Charles climbed in the car with me and began a litany of his travels that day. He had decided that his wife was in dire need of a doctor, so he arose early and walked down the mountain to New River, rowed a boat across the river and hitch-hiked to Hinton. The state of traffic along that road was meager in those days and he ended up walking most of the 12 or so miles. When he got to Hinton he was unable to find Dr. Stokes, a physician that frequently made calls into the Richmond District. No other doctor there would even consider the trip, so Charles hitch-hiked back down the road, rowed back across the river and walked up the mountain to check on his wife.

He made her comfortable and walked on up the mountain to the village of Abraham, found somebody with a truck that would take him part of the way out, where he caught another ride to Beaver, and there I entered the picture. All told, Charles had walked about twenty miles since before daybreak. He related the story without rancor or self pity. It was just one of those matter of fact, day to day happenings to a person who is used to living on the edge of nowhere.

The highway narrowed into a single paved lane after we passed the Water Company dam.

"I tried to call from there but weren't nobody home," Charles said, pointing to the caretaker's house, as we drove by. In time I would become used to hearing the Kessingers' voices as they made calls for the people beyond the reach of Ma Bell.

The narrow paved road ended abruptly at the old log church at Pluto, and became a gravel road. In time the gravel turned to rocks and ruts and I would wince at the sound of the bottom of my 1950 Buick Special dragging over the high spots in the road. Houses became few and far between. Charles called out the names of the residents as we passed. Some places were rough looking houses, not much more than cabins. Others were handsome, substantial, well-kept farm houses, surrounded by wide pastures and crop fields.

We passed through Abraham, and I was beginning to recall some landmarks. The road was climbing slightly once again and I could see the crest of a hill off to the right. A peaked roof was visible just over the horizon.

"Stop here," Charles said. "We can't drive to the house, but hit tain't but a step over there."

We walked the short distance up the hill and followed the path down toward the gate. A wagon road turned off to the left, and Charles followed the road. I looked back with dismay at the disappearing house.

Some distance down the road, another path dropped off to the right into the woods.

"We'll take a shortcut down this path. Cuts off pert near half mile."

That path was steep! My medical bag was getting heavier. The sun was unmercifully hot. My temper was rising as I considered the statement about it being "just a step over there."

We broke out of the woods into a valley lined with peach trees, weighted down with ripe fruit. A creek gurgled over rocks at the edge of the small orchard.

"That's Farley's Creek. Used to be a sight of mountain trout in that creek. T'aint many left. I catch a mess once in a while," Charles said, nonchalantly.

It began to come back to me; we had walked down the mountain years before on a similarly hot day, but in a less accessible area, and, exhausted, we had dropped flat on our backs in the creek. We didn't catch any fish. To top off the day, we couldn't find the path which we had followed to the creek, and had to climb up the side of the mountain. Just the words, "Farley's Creek," made me seethe.

The house sat at the head of the valley. It was a neat frame house, devoid of paint, sparsely furnished, sitting in a yard of swept dirt, not a blade of grass to be seen anywhere. Chickens pecked away at the dirt, and scattered before us as we walked through the yard.

Mrs. Kincaid was in the midst of a hard chill. Quilts were piled over her, yet the temperature outside the house was close to 90°. Her temperature was 104°. Her pulse rate was slow, not in keeping with a fever such as she had.

It wasn't easy to examine her. She kept pulling the quilts tight around her feverish body that was shaking violently, but I could see the faint, scattered rash over her chest and abdomen that blanched to pressure. She flinched when I palpated her enlarged spleen.

In years past, when medicine was more an art and less a science, odors were associated with diseases. Dr. Austin Flint at the University of Pennsylvania in the late nineteenth century, and the revered

Sir William Osler, made reference to various odors being associated with certain diseases. The odor of bananas was often associated with typhoid, which we now know as being due to the formation of ketones (acetone) from the dehydration that accompanied the disease. I was aware of the odor.

"Where do you get your water, Charles," I asked.

"Spring. Comes right out of the hill, just up behind the house."

We walked up to the spring. Animal tracks surrounded the spring–dogs, pigs, a cow and chickens. Flies buzzed through the open door of the outhouse, which was just off to the side. I could see their flight path back and forth toward the open, unscreened windows of the house. Also, though it was some distance, the farm that we had passed in our walk was up there somewhere.

Now came the dilemma. What was I going to do with the patient? There was apparently no way to get the patient out of the hollow. I did have a bottle of Chloramphenicol, a relatively new antibiotic that was highly effective against the typhoid bacillus. It had been a welcoming gift from the representative of Pfizer Pharmaceutical, the manufacturer of the drug.

I drew some blood to send to the State Health Department for an agglutination test to confirm the diagnosis, left the bottle of capsules, along with instructions about diet, liquids, and cold compresses for fever, and a promise that I would be back in a couple of days to check on things, a trip that I didn't look forward to with eagerness.

Charles walked with me to the orchard, where the "shortcut" path headed up the mountain.

"How much I owe you, Doc?"

Earlier, about halfway down the mountain, and getting angrier at each step, I had determined that I was going to charge him one hundred dollars.

I said, "Twenty dollars?" with some trepidation, and I was prepared to defend it.

Charles pulled his wallet out of his overalls. It was held closed with a rubber band that had been cut from an inner tube, and when he slipped the band free, the packed wallet sprung open. He searched through the bills for a twenty, pulled one part way out and then shoved it back.

"Let me get you a clean one," he said. The other one was crisp.

He thanked me and then offered me a bushel of peaches. I declined with the explanation that I couldn't carry them up the mountain.

"Oh, I'll tote 'em up to your car. Be glad to."

I allowed as how I wouldn't think of his walking up there again just to carry me a basket of peaches. I took two to eat along the way.

It was almost eight o'clock when I got home.

I called the County Health Department the next morning to report the case. My brother-in-law was the acting health officer and I think he was a bit dubious about my diagnosis, but he was going to send the Health Department nurses out there. I gave him directions about how to get there and added, "Have them park right there at the house. They'll see the peak of a roof from the road. It's just a step over the hill." They made the trip wearing their neat, blue uniforms, nylons, and dainty, navy blue pumps. My

14

reputation with the County nurses was damaged forever.

I went back two days later and found Mrs. Kincaid much improved, to my great relief. Her agglutination titer had been very high, over 2000. I was rather smug that my diagnosis had been correct. But I was not yet through with the Kincaid family.

About a week later the hospital called and said there was a man up there with his daughter that wanted to see me. It was Charles. His daughter had been out of the hollow visiting when she got sick. Since transportation was available, he had brought her into the hospital.

She had been vomiting and was pretty well dehydrated. I wanted to admit her but Charles said no. His wife had done so well that he thought I should give her some of the same medicine, and he would take her home. I did convince him that the girl should have some IV fluids. That was done, and I gave him a prescription for some Chloramphenicol to have filled at the drugstore, and promised him that I would come out to check on things in a couple of days.

They had gotten a neighbor who had a Jeep to haul the daughter into the hollow. When I went back two days later, she was much improved, and the mother was greatly improved and able to be up.

Charles walked with me to the path again and paid my fee. I had reduced it to ten dollars by then because there was a farm pond not far from where I parked that had a population of some fabulous bass.

"Doc, I don't see how you can do this so cheap. That medicine I got at the drugstore was same as you give my old lady, but it cost me over sixty dollars, and then I had to pay the hospital for that stuff you give the girl in her blood veins. You been out here four times and it still ain't cost that much."

Every year, along late in the summer when the peaches were ripe, a bushel of peaches appeared on the porch. I knew who put them there.

≈ ≈

∞4∞

THE ONLOOKER SYNDROME

I suspect all young doctors feel that they must sometimes make an effort to look as if they are doing something heroic in a time of emergency, even when they know it is useless, but especially when onlookers dictate by their expressions of expectation that such an effort will be made. It is known as the Onlooker Syndrome. I was no different when my turn came.

The Highway Department began widening the small concrete bridge that crossed Beaver Creek. It caused a lot of traffic problems going to and from my office. I surveyed the progress as I passed by. It was encouraging to see the dragline scooping out rocks and gravel for the wider, more substantial bridge.

I had just gotten home and settled down with the afternoon paper to rest for a few moments before dinner, when the phone rang. It was the man who ran a small beer joint beside the bridge. His voice was urgent!

"Doc! They need you down at the bridge right away. Been a man done got electrocuted." The phone went dead before I could get any more information. I assumed that it was the bridge under construction.

It was about two miles from my home to the bridge. The first mile was easy. Traffic was backed up for the next mile, some of the cars were trying to turn around, others were parked at odd angles while the occupants ran up the road to see what exciting event had happened. I finally made my way to the scene.

The man had been standing in the creek directing the bucket of the dragline that was scooping out the creek, where the footers for the bridge pier would be poured. The boom of the shovel had touched a high voltage cable at the same time that the man had touched the bucket.

I asked how long it had been since the accident. Fifteen minutes, some said. Another man said twenty minutes at least. Another man looked at his wrist and agreed. I did notice that he did not have a wrist watch. Everyone looked at me expectantly.

I listened carefully for a heartbeat . . . nothing. The expectant looks continued. I checked his pupils, dilated and non-reactive, always a bad sign. The expectant looks were even more intense. I opened my bag and took out an ampule of epinephrine and a syringe. The crowd grew silent except for the shuffle of feet as various ones pushed in closer. Murmurs of hushed voices were heard as I sucked up some adrenaline from the ampule. There was a sudden drawing in of breaths when I attached the long needle to the syringe. Gasps were heard as I pushed the needle through the chest wall into the heart and drew back dark blood from the ventricle. The cold body relaxed and exhaled a final sigh. One of the more enraptured onlookers, who was kneeling at the head of the victim, looked up at me and grinned.

"By Gawd, that got 'im, didn't it Doc," he said.

⚘5⚘

ADVENTURES IN OBSTETRICS

Obstetrics is a fascinating part of the practice of medicine, especially in family practice where you are aware of the entire family and their situation. The prenatal visits of the expectant mother are very much like watching a garden grow. If the delivery was to take place at home, as many of them did in those days, it was often an adventure.

Generally there was an older woman present, a "Granny," not necessarily a grandmother, but of course many of them were, even if not so related to the patient. A Granny was a woman who came in to help, to organize, to oversee the "birthing." Often the expectant mother would inform me that 'so and so' is going to Granny me," hence the term. Some women had a special reputation as a Granny and were much sought after.

My first experience with a particularly austere and formidable Granny came on a cold, fall night. This was about the fifth or sixth child, and the prenatal course had gone well. The expectant mother had been very cooperative and I was in a very good mood as I bounced through the darkness to the home, and whistling as I went up onto the porch and was admitted by the unfamiliar Granny.

The Granny looked at me coldly and said, "Doctors don't whistle." I cringed inwardly. She had just gotten in the driver's seat.

I spoke with the mother-to-be, and asked about her husband. I felt the need for male support. He was off coon hunting. "He came back from calling you, and said he'd seen this big raccoon crossing the road, and he was going to take his hounds and see if they could pick up the trail," the patient said. The Granny gave a disgusted sniff of displeasure.

Examination revealed that the mother-to-be was fine, contractions were regular, fetal heart was good, and the cervix was dilated about five centimeters. It would not be a long case. I got things ready and sat down in a rocking chair in the next room and rocked slowly. Each time I would rock forward I could see the glaring face of the Granny burning through the dim light. It was discomfiting.

Periodically I would get up from my chair and check the contractions for length and frequency, and listen to the fetal heart. I was aware of a sniff of displeasure each time I did my checkup.

Finally the mother began to moan and to writhe about, an almost sure sign of imminent delivery. The head was visible as I pulled on my gloves and draped the patient.

The Granny took her place near the head of the patient.

"Is it time to quill her?" she asked, in a precise, determined voice.

I tried not to give her a questioning look. "No, not yet," I said. She gave another sniff of displeasure.

There was another hard contraction, and the mother let out a small cry of pain.

"Now can I quill her?" the Granny asked, almost frantically.

The head was now crowning and I could see no contraindication to doing whatever it was that she was so insistent on, so I said, "Yes."

She drew a long feather from her apron pocket

and began tickling the mother's nose. It was only moments until she sneezed and the baby was propelled into the world like a cannonball. Quick hands and the umbilical cord prevented the baby from going over the foot of the bed.

I clamped and cut the cord, delivered the placenta and never mentioned the effect of the "quilling." The Granny cleaned up the baby and said nothing. As a matter of fact our entire conversation that night had concerned only whistling and quilling.

By the time I had repacked all of my instruments and examined the baby, the Granny was busy putting on a pot of coffee. "Set yourself down there and have a cup of this coffee," she ordered. "I don't allow the doctor to leave for at least an hour after the birthing."

I assured her I wasn't leaving.

The father came in from coon hunting, and hung up his red, plaid hunting coat beside the door, and went into the bedroom to check on his wife and new daughter.

"How're you feeling?" he asked.

"Oh I feel fine. It gets easier all the time," she said. "Did you get the coon?"

He had, and it was a big one. The dogs had worked great, he told her.

Dawn was just beginning to break over the Glade Creek gorge as I started for the door. The Granny followed me, her eyes twinkling. "You didn't know what I meant about quilling, did you?"

I confessed that I had no idea. From there on we were friends and shared many hours of waiting together for "the birthing."

Somewhere in my training it had been stressed that on home deliveries the doctor should not leave the home for at least an hour. The Granny reminded me of it. Later another Granny told me the same thing, and to back up her conviction about the doctor not rushing off, she related this story.

"I was out at the Clarks' place when their first baby was born. It was a fine boy. She'd had a hard time though. Almost twenty-four hours, and she was pretty bad wore out. The doctor packed up and left as soon as he could get his stuff together.

"He hadn't been gone but about a half-hour when she started bleeding. I told Mr. Clark that he better get on his horse and catch that doctor. 'Your wife's a-bleedin' to death,' I said.

"He got his horse and took out after the doctor and caught him about six miles down the road. He said 'Doc, come back, my wife's a-hemorrhaging.' And you know what that doctor said? He said, 'Clark, if she was hemorrhaging when you left, ain't no use me going back there. She's dead.' And when Mr. Clark got home, sure enough, she was."

Though I had been taught that you didn't leave for at least an hour, that story made a profound impression on me, especially when I later came to know Mr. Clark.

~

My predecessor had taken on some obstetrical patients, done their prenatal care, and had told them that I would be their doctor.

Some of them had even "prepaid" a portion of the fee for obstetrical care, which at that time was 35 dollars. It included prenatal care, with the exception of the necessary laboratory work: serology for syphilis as required by state law, complete blood count, RH factor, which was just becoming routine, and a chest X-ray. If it was the first baby, very often in the last month of pregnancy X-ray pelvimetry, (a measurement of the pelvic outlet of the mother), was obtained. Attorneys today would have a fit trying to say that this or that congenital malformation was due to exposure from radiation. Actually I think we saw less congenital malformation then we do now.

The patient that I was going to see on this particular summer evening, a week or so after beginning my practice, was one of those that the doctor had promised my services. I had not seen her for a prenatal visit before being called, so I stopped by the office to check her record. I was distressed to find that this was her first baby and I had not intended to deliver first babies in the home, but it was too late now to inform her of that.

It was a warm evening and near dusk when I drove up to the house. In the distance I could hear thunder rolling in a dense cloud bank to the west. Birds were twittering on their roosts, except for a thrush that was trilling an evening song in a bush near where my car had stopped.

The house was rustic, apparently fairly new. The unpainted lumber smelled almost sawmill fresh. On the porch a small, short-haired dog yapped a nervous warning beside the patient's father, who was waiting anxiously for my arrival. He wanted me to come in quickly. The dog didn't even want me on the porch. The patient's mother scooped up the dog and disappeared into the house with it. The dog was too little to sound vicious, but he certainly knew how to make a person feel unwelcome.

I introduced myself to the soon-to-be grandfather and grandmother. Inside I found a soon-to-be great-grandmother, aunt, mother-in-law and, most pitiful of all, the father-to-be, who, if there had been Lamaze classes at that time, most certainly would have flunked out. It was going to be a real show, I could tell.

The patient was in a low brass bed with a thin mattress, and when I stood beside the bed the top of the mattress was just level with my knees. The patient didn't look old enough to have started menstruating, much less have a baby. She was seventeen, and the father was eighteen.

She had been in labor most of the day, but the great-grandmother-to-be had thought it unnecessary to call me until the membranes ruptured, or as she put it, "Her bag of waters broke."

I came face to face with reality when I examined her. The baby was in a frank breech position and the cervix was almost completely dilated. Furthermore, we were almost fifteen miles from the nearest hospital, and about half of that was on a dirt road that would soon be nearly impassable, judging by the sound of the large rain drops that were beginning to pelt the metal roof. I was also alarmed to find that her blood pressure was 170/105, and her feet were very edematous. Both were fairly good evidence of the toxemia of pregnancy, preeclampsia.

Toxemia of pregnancy was an ancient term that originated when it was believed that certain "toxins" formed in the pregnant woman's body that interfered with various systems, especially renal function. The resulting retention of fluids produce a generalized edema, including cerebral edema. Along with an elevation of blood pressure, it can be a severe, at times life-threatening, situation to the mother and to the baby. Eclampsia, or convulsive seizures, often resulted. In this case it was termed preeclampsia. In other words, the convulsion was a possibility. In most cases, once the baby is delivered, the mother usually recovers from the problems.

I found myself remembering back to a night when I was a junior medical student on the obstetrical service. A lady was in labor, and near delivery, when it was discovered that she had a breech presentation. The Chief of OB was present, and the Chief Resident. All of the students on the floor were rounded up and assembled in the delivery room to observe the skill of the Chief Resident in delivering a breech birth.

The body came out fine, as it generally does. The Resident was going to use Piper forceps to deliver the "aftercoming head," as it is spoken of in the textbooks. The only trouble was, the arms were crossed above the head.

"You must bring down the arms first," the Professor said. "Just hook your finger over the arm, turn the baby slightly to that side and bring the arm down. Then do the same thing with the other arm."

The Resident did as he was told and with the first arm we heard a muffled snap. He had broken the humerus. He hooked the other arm, and twisting the little body slightly, just like it said in the textbook, he pulled down and snapped that arm.

By then the baby was blue from lack of oxygen. That's the bad part about breech births–the baby's chest is compressed by delivery, making it hard for the baby to breath. The head must be delivered quickly.

25

He finally got the forceps on and completed the delivery. It wasn't even a big baby. I thought it was dead. So did the other students.

The Professor had it placed in an incubator with an endotracheal tube in place, attached to oxygen that flowed through a manually operated respirator. The operators of the respirator were junior medical students on the OB service, night and day, around the clock, two hours on, eight hours off, for the next three days, at which time the Professor and the Chief Resident felt that they had done enough to establish the fact that the baby was beyond saving.

On an examination later, one of the questions was: List the indications for Caesarean Section. As I recall there were about four or five at the time. I added another one: Breech Presentation. It was marked with a big red slash and the word NO! written beside it. It is an accepted indication today.

There was not that option for me this night. I also didn't have Piper forceps, which probably was in my favor, and certainly in the baby's favor. Fortunately I had the opportunity to deliver a breech baby when I was an Intern, and it turned out okay. I was praying that my luck was going to hold out.

The body came out slick as a whistle. The arms were not extended over the head. The Giffard maneuver, slipping the middle finger into the baby's mouth, and the index and ring fingers against the baby's cheek bones, allowed me to slide the head out with ease. The baby took a deep breath and cried. Just then the lightning struck the transformer beside the house with a loud boom, and all the lights went out.

The women all screamed. The poor father came running in, wrung out, certain that the trumpet of Gabriel had blown before he ever had a chance to see his progeny. The grandfather found a flashlight and gave it to the now great-grandmother to hold while he rounded up an oil lamp.

I delivered the placenta just before the patient began twitching with the beginning of a convulsion. I had the medication to contract the uterus already drawn up in a syringe and I got that into her, but I couldn't massage the uterus to stimulate contraction and take care of the convulsion also.

The new Daddy was up on the bed beside his wife and sobbing, certain that he was about to become a widower. I showed him how to massage the uterus to help it contract and then fumbled through my bag for some Nembutal for the convulsion. The worse part was getting great-grandma to hold the flashlight still while I searched. She kept flashing it around the room to make sure everybody was present and accounted for.

I got a needle into a vein, injected the Nembutal, and the convulsion ceased. The Daddy had done an admirable job and the uterus was well contracted. I heaved a sigh of relief.

Grandpa had gone into the pantry to find an oil lamp, and the little, yapping dog had slipped by him and came tearing into the room, convinced that I was the culprit that was the cause of all of the confusion, and began tearing at my pants leg. He was too small to do much damage, but I was in no mood to play kindly, dog-loving doctor, and I shoved him with my foot. Well, maybe the word shoved is understating it, but considering what I was going through at the time, that little yapper was lucky to be able to run howling into the living room. He was followed by great-grandma and the flashlight, she uttering endearing terms and phrases about his character, and much less complimentary terms about mine.

Finally Grandpa showed up with a lamp, great-grandma came back, glowering at me, but at least she had the flashlight and continued flashing it about like a disoriented firefly, to make certain that all of the participants were present, except me. I was on her blacklist.

Because of the low bed, I had to kneel on the floor in order to sew up the episiotomy, slipping in a stitch when the flashlight beam passed by. The light of an oil lamp isn't exactly Delivery Room quality.

The little mother did fine. Her blood pressure was a respectable 140/85. The uterus was firm. The episiotomy repair looked decent, considering what I went through to get it that way. The baby was squalling vigorously and making sucking sounds on his fist.

"I'll fix him some catnip tea," great-grandma said, and went into the kitchen.

The minute the door opened, the dog came tearing for my leg again and everybody but me began grabbing at him. I was poised and ready if he got close enough.

Catnip was commonly used by various Grannies. It was supposed to "cut the phlegm" so the baby could breath better, and also act as a stimulant. From the way this baby was squalling, he didn't need a stimulant.

The following morning I walked into the office, slightly bent over from the night before. Bessie grinned.

"These home deliveries really do get to your back, don't they," she said. She didn't even know the half of it.

~

There was one delivery in which I was probably in the most miserable circumstance possible.

The mother was fairly near term when she came to me. I agreed to take her as a patient, but with reluctance. It was one of those times that instinct tells you NO, in capital letters, and you don't listen.

The snow was deep, and it crackled under my feet because of the near zero temperature of the February night. The stars sparkled overhead, a good sign that it was going to become even colder. Just the short distance that I walked from the car to the house made me anticipate the warmth I was expecting inside.

The "house" was in reality an old store building. I knocked heavily on the door several times before I was admitted by a young woman, a stranger to me. The old counter and some shelves showed eerily in the light reflected from the snow through the dusty windows.

My guide led me into another large, cold, mostly empty room, and off to the side was a smaller room, just large enough for a bed, a chair, and a pot-bellied stove that was glowing with heat, marvelous heat. The bed contained the woman in labor, and my guide dropped down into the single chair beside the stove, a platform rocker with a comforting creak. It was crowded in the room and I had difficulty finding a place to set my OB bag, and to move about while I examined the patient to determine the progress of labor. The mother and her friend seemed much more interested in their conversation about neighbors, most of which was not complimentary, then the situation at hand.

With that part of my job done, I looked about for a place to sit and wait. Obviously it wasn't going to be in that room. I looked into the large room. It was lit by a single light bulb hanging from the ceiling. I could read 40W against its feeble effort to provide illumination. At the far end of the room, much too far to gain any effect from the glowing fire in the bedroom, there was a straight chair and a cookstove. A woodbox beside the stove held a dozen or so sticks of knotty pine kindling and some old newspapers.

With my overcoat on, and out of the wind, I thought I might not freeze, providing the delivery was fairly quick. I paced up and down to keep my circulation going, and finally, in desperation, built a fire in the stove. A few sheets of newspaper and three sticks of knotty pine doesn't go a long way, but at least I could detect some heat, and eventually there was warmth in the oven. I opened the oven door and sat on it and let my back soak up what heat it could, and listened enviously to the creaking of the platform rocker beside the stove in the other room.

Once I went to check the patient, and they reluctantly paused in their conversation. It was difficult to examine her because her friend didn't want to move out of the way. She was probably afraid I would grab her chair.

Labor was progressing, but not fast enough.

Back to my fire. It was almost to the dying ember stage. Cautiously, I added a few more sticks of wood and sat on the oven door again.

I must have dozed off because I was startled by a piercing scream from the other room, the warm one. The mother had reached the stage of labor that we as medical students always called the "Lord-Jesus-help-me" stage. Obstetrical texts do not mention this stage of labor. It frequently includes various threats as to what is going to happen to him who caused this situation.

At last a chance to be warm. I hurried to the room. Indeed she was fully dilated and the head was beginning to crown. I informed the friend that she was going to have to get out of the chair and make room for the task at hand, and grudgingly she obliged.

The baby was healthy. From somewhere hot water appeared and the friend cleaned up the baby and the mother. It seemed that in another little corner of the old building was another room with real light, a real stove, with real fire, that they hadn't mentioned.

As I filled out the information in the little book that the Health Department provided so a Birth Certificate could be made, and came to the part for the address of the father, the friend informed me that he was in the Penitentiary for voluntary manslaughter, and had wanted it made known to the doctor that delivered his baby, that if anything went wrong, he was going to come looking for that doctor when he got out of the Pen. I examined the baby very carefully, again.

When I got back in my car, the heater wouldn't work.

~

I was called for one delivery on a patient that I had seen for prenatal care but about whose home

31

situation I knew nothing. Had I known about the house before, I might not have been there to deliver this baby.

It was a hot summer day when she went into labor, and as usual the house was way out in the country. It was a small, four room dwelling, sitting in the middle of a field, and the sun was beating down with a vengeance as I drove into the yard. Two children, about two and three, maybe four years of age, were playing in the dirt. They didn't even look up.

I walked into the house through an unscreened door, and called, "Anybody home?"

"In here," a voice directed me to the bedroom.

The bedroom was small, just large enough to hold a bed and have enough room to walk beside it. Hanging directly over the bed, on the side where the patient was lying, was a long coil of flypaper which the flies were successfully avoiding. The room was sweltering! I heard a vehicle rattle into the yard. Help, I hoped.

The patient was lying under a quilt. I turned the cover back to examine her, and flies from miles around zoomed in. The membranes had ruptured and she was lying in a pool of amniotic fluid. It appeared that it had been a while since the membranes had ruptured. I checked her quickly and shooed all the flies out, I hoped, and covered her up again.

The flies retreated to the ceiling, avoiding the long tube of flypaper a lot better than I did.

"Call me when you feel the baby coming," I said, and retreated to the porch.

It was the husband who had driven up. He was now sitting on the edge of the porch, whittling

32

on a stick, and spitting tobacco juice at chickens that came into range. One unsuspecting pullet pecked its way toward the porch and he nailed it with a long string of juice.

"Hot damn! Got 'im," he said. He looked up at me, squinting his eyes against the bright sky. "Hot," he said. I agreed.

"Is anyone going to help out here?" I asked.

"Miz Smith, down the road a piece, said she'd come," he said.

"Have you gone to tell her it's time?"

"Yep."

"When's she coming?"

"She ain't home."

"Well, you better get busy then and have things ready because you're going to have a lot to do very shortly, like washing and dressing a baby, cleaning up the bed and your wife, and disposing of some afterbirth."

That last duty galvanized him into action. He jumped up and ran to his pickup, saying something about trying to find somebody. In about twenty minutes he was back with a woman who looked capable, even if she didn't appear to be greatly motivated. She did get some semblance of order in the house though.

Finally the mother called out that the baby was coming. I went into the bedroom. "Is it here yet?" I asked.

"I think the head is, anyhow," she said.

I had the new Granny turn back the quilt. I extracted the rest of the baby, clamped and cut the cord, lifted the baby out of the bed, got my head caught in the flypaper, and shooed out the flies, all in about 30 seconds.

While the Granny was taking care of the baby, I massaged the fundus of the uterus until the placenta came loose. Once more I uncovered the patient, retrieved the placenta, shooed out the flies, and got caught in the flypaper again. I put the placenta in a bucket and carried it out onto the porch, followed by a long string of flies.

Daddy was nowhere to be seen. The children were still playing in the dirt. When I left about an hour later, the situation was unchanged, except the flies had been on a recruiting mission.

≈ ∽

≈6≈

THE MAN WHO DEFEATED THE GERM THEORY

It was a hot, sultry day when I first met Roscoe. He had been brought in by Everett, a local man who hired him from time to time to do odd jobs. The purpose of the visit was to have him examined in order to get him on Welfare.

Everett came into the examining room with him and answered most of the questions. Roscoe helped out by responding to each of Everett's answers by saying, "Yep."

Roscoe was dressed in jeans and a shirt that had never seen a washtub. Neither had Roscoe. He was wearing high-top, laced, rubber boots.

I filled out the questionnaire as best I could, hoping that the "Yep" uttered by Roscoe confirmed every answer that Everett had given.

I said, "Take your clothes off."

Roscoe looked at me, his head turned slightly to one side, and angled in a downward position, so that he could focus at least one eye in my direction. Both eyes were distracted by the worst case of divergent strabismus that I had ever seen.

"Boots too?" he asked.

Everett jumped up off the stool he had been perched on.

"I'm leaving," he said.

Roscoe took off his boots and the odor began permeating the room. It was stifling, overwhelming, noxious to the point of nausea. I did the quickest physical exam of my life. It is still a record.

After Roscoe and Everett left, Bessie and I opened all the windows and doors and left for lunch and house calls. When I returned Bessie had placed deodorizing wicks about the office in strategic places. The one in the examining room had wilted from overwork.

I had seen Roscoe and his family numerous times walking along the highway, going to and from the store, or post office. They didn't walk together. Roscoe was always in front, and several paces ahead of the rest of the family. He was followed by his wife, who carried the baby, and then the five older children. If they were on the way home from the store, the children were ladened with bags. Occasionally the wife carried a bag or two, and the oldest child carried the baby. Roscoe carried nothing. Sometimes, if the load was particularly heavy and the caravan was wearing down, Roscoe would be as much as a hundred feet or so in the lead.

The first time I was called to their house was to see Mrs. Roscoe. The house was three rooms, the middle room being the entrance and occupied by a bed and a dresser. To the right was another room, separated by a door with slats nailed up to a height of perhaps three feet. The room was very small, more of a walk-in closet. There was no furniture, just a pile of old quilts and blankets jumbled up on the floor.

The room to the left was obviously the kitchen with a coal stove to cook on, a rickety kitchen cabinet, a dry sink full of dirty dishes and a rough plank table with benches to either side. The table was covered with dirty dishes that had not been promoted to a place in the dry sink. One slat-bottomed chair stood at the head of the table.

Four children of various ages stood at the doorway into the closet-sized room, with the same wide-eyed, strained expressions of curiosity that calves have when they stand at a fence watching some out of the ordinary event.

Mrs. Roscoe was stretched out on the bed. She had vomited several times on the floor beside the bed, and apparently wiped her mouth and hands on her dress each time.

Beside her on the bed was a child of about ten months, wearing only a shirt and no diaper, and her bottom had not been cleaned since the last diaper she had messed. It appeared to have been some time ago. She was mostly asleep and clutching a bottle that contained what appeared to be milk.

"Roscoe, I thought I told you to put this baby to bed," Mrs. Roscoe yelled.

Roscoe picked the little girl up by an arm and one leg, carried her over to the "pen" and tossed her into the pile of quilts. She landed with a dull thump.

A muffled voice uttered an oath, "Shit!" and a rumpled, tousled head that appeared to be about four years of age popped up, rearranged itself, and went back to sleep. The baby momentarily lost her grasp on the bottle, whimpered as she fumbled in the covers until she found it, and poked the grimy nipple into her mouth. She gave a contented sigh and went back to sleep. The other children continued their calf-like stares.

I examined Mrs. Roscoe. She was short and fat. She was not having any pain. She said that even the smell of food made her nauseous, and caused her to vomit. Roscoe agreed.

"I keep trying to git her to fix me a bite to eat but all she does is puke," Roscoe complained. "I ain't been able to git a lick of work done for all the house-work I had to do."

Examination didn't enlighten the situation any. I had one more question, and I dreaded to ask because I had a feeling what the answer would be.

"When was your last period," I asked.

She hadn't had one since the baby was born. She would not have another until after the next one was born.

It was after that house call that I began to have doubts about the germ theory.

I had made a call to Roscoe's house to see some of the children. Three of the children were in school, and from all reports were surprisingly good students. There were several cases of scarlatina in the school, and now there were two more cases. I lined up all the children on the bed in the middle room and gave them injections of penicillin, then had them jump back in the pen. I figured the others would eventually get it, so I started treatment early. I gave instructions about keeping them quiet, diet, and control of fever. I suggested that gargling might help to ease their throats, but from the expression on the parents' faces, I doubted that this would ever happen. I promised to return the next day to give them more penicillin.

I made another call, and returned to the office. The Principal of the school was on the phone.

"Doc," he said, his voice betraying his feeling of fear, "I just got a note from Roscoe that said two of his children have the smallpox. Good God, man, what can we do?"

I calmed him down with the truth.

I had no more than hung up the phone when it rang again. It was a County Health Nurse. Roscoe had run up the road to Everett's place of business, stood out on the road and yelled in to him that he wasn't going to be able to work for a while because there was smallpox in his house. Everett, in turn, called the Health Department to see if there were any precautions he should take for himself and the other employees.

The following day, when I went back to give the children more penicillin, I was greeted by a big sign nailed to a tree beside the path up to the house:

KEEP OUT
SMALLPOX
DOC BANKS SAYS ITS SO

Roscoe came into the office asking for some sleeping medicine. He said his wife couldn't sleep, and it kept him awake with all her tossing and turning. I explained to him that it wouldn't be good for her to take any sleeping medicine, that it might hurt the baby.

Roscoe cocked his head over to one side and looked me in the eye, or at least in that general vicinity, and said, "Hell it ain't fer the old lady, it fer me, so's she won't keep me awake."

Mrs. Roscoe had her baby. I insisted that it had to be born in the hospital. There was no way that I would ever attempt a delivery in that house. By that time they had gotten a Medical Card from the Department of Welfare, and it was well deserved.

It was a boy. I came down from the Delivery Room to tell Roscoe, who was waiting in the lobby.

A couple of other expectant fathers had gone outside to wait. The clerk in the business office had closed the little pass-through window over her desk. Roscoe's presence was detectable from some distance down the corridor.

I gave him the news and asked him what he was going to name the baby.

"Gonna call him Roscoe, Jr."

I said, "You can't call him that; you already have a Roscoe, Jr."

Roscoe adjusted his head so that one of his divergent eyes could focus on me.

"I know. I know. He's such a good boy, I'm gonna name this kid after him. We'll name him Junior Roscoe, Jr."

I don't know what happened when the certificate got to the State Department of Health.

It was not many months later that Roscoe and his family moved away, and I never saw any of them again as patients. The house in which they had been living was condemned and burned.

Over a year later I was making a house call in an abandoned mining town and was just getting into my car when I saw Roscoe.

The house in which they were living was on the hillside, just above the road. It was a late winter afternoon and slushy, gray snow covered most of the ground. Snow that is gray from coal dust is what you see in mining towns. The houses were most always painted gray. On a cold, gray day, the grayness seeps into your mind and everything you see blends into the slush. It is a depressing scene. Seeing Roscoe made it more so.

He was standing on the back porch of this old company house, bundled in an old, worn and ragged overcoat. A cap was held over his head with a muffler tied beneath his chin. He was being handed a plate of food and a cup of steaming something or the other, coffee I suppose, through a window. I watched as he carried it back to his shelter which appeared to be a bunch of old boards, arranged lean-to fashion, and covered with a piece of a tarpaulin. He turned the tarpaulin back and crawled in, apparently banished from the house by his family.

≈7≈

THE MUSTARD SEED

*"For if you had faith even
as small as a tiny mustard seed,
you could say to the mountain,
'Move,' and it would go far away.
Nothing would be impossible."*
Matthew 17:20

Milt was a large, barrel-chested man. In his younger days I think he was barrel-chested from raw strength. Now his chest was shaped so from the ravages of emphysema, the result of too many cigarettes and the dust of too many coal mines. His lips were a dusky blue and the fingers of his spatulate hands resembled ball bats. His nail beds matched his lips.

Milt sat mostly in an upholstered chair that had conformed itself to his bulk, with a piece of rubber tubing hanging from his mouth. A tank of oxygen stood behind the chair, forcing its contents through the tube that connected it to Milt. Coiled up beside the tank was an extra length of tubing that he could attach to make himself more mobile, at least enough length to get to the bathroom. More than once, when I would stop by while his wife was at work, I would find the tubing snaking its way across the room and around a corner. I would wait and shortly Milt would appear, winding up the tubing, and with his usual broad grin through blue lips that were stretched across his face.

Milt would drop down into his chair, pant and cough and wheeze. I often sat and listened for far too long a time to his tales of Blue Jay, another town that timbering built and where my father had practiced fifty years ago. Milt had done it all; felled trees, worked in the mill, fired on the dinky engine that hauled trees out of the mountains, and then moved on into the mines. From the expression on his face, and the sound of his voice as he related his tales, it was obvious that he had enjoyed each moment.

Finally the day came that I thought Milt should be in the hospital. He had developed pneumonia, and his heart was laboring under the stress of trying to provide oxygen that was in short supply to lungs too scarred to expand, lungs even more compromised by the congestion produced by the infection.

Despite everything that could be done, Milt was slipping away. I checked on him late one night and silently said good-bye as I left his room. A private duty nurse was standing beside his bed.

"Call me," I said. She nodded in response.

I stopped by the house and sat with his wife for a time, drinking coffee and trying to answer her questions as best I could. I explained that I did not expect Milt to make it through the night. She understood. I think.

I slept fitfully. Part of it was the coffee, but mostly it was from expecting the phone to ring.

I was up early and off to the hospital without breakfast. Milt's room was my first stop. He was sitting up in bed eating breakfast, the oxygen tent pushed back. A huge grin passed over his face as I entered the room. He stuck out his hand.

"Sit down Doc, I got to talk to you." I sat down and he continued talking, not gasping, not wheezing, not coughing. The only thing that interrupted his voice was eating.

"Doc, I had a dream last night," he said. "I dreamed that I was at a funeral. It was over at Blue Jay where the old church stands on the hill?" He said it as a question and looked at me to see if I knew the place. I nodded.

"Years ago there was a big stump behind the church. Must've been at least eight foot across. The women always spread tablecloths over it when we had outdoor dinners. It's gone now I expect." I tried to picture it. Did I remember it, or did I just want to remember it?

"Well, this time there wasn't no dinner on it. There was a body lying there, all shrouded up. My Mother and Daddy were standing there looking, all my kinfolks that have been dead for years was standing there looking. Then it was when I realized that the dead person lying there was me, and I was up above looking down." His voice choked slightly and his eyes filled with tears. "Just then there was a loud, booming voice that said, 'There'll be no death for Milt Shumaker tonight,' and I woke up."

I didn't doubt his story. The fact that he was alive, sitting up in bed, eating breakfast, no oxygen hissing into the tent, and less cyanotic then I had ever seen him, was sufficient evidence to convince me that something very much out of the ordinary had occurred. I read the nurses notes in his chart. They went something like this:

1:10 AM   Pt. Dyspneic, restless, coughing.
               Suctioned thick mucous. Pulse 135,
               weak.

1:30 AM   Restless, cyanotic. O_2 at 8 L Suctioned.
               Pulse 155, weak, irreg.

1:45 AM   Cond. Unchgd

2:00 AM   Very restless. Dyspneic. BP 110/50, P 160 cont. irreg. R 32, shallow.

2:15 AM   Suctioned heavy mucous. Cyanotic. R 35 P 160 irreg. BP 100/50

2:30 AM   Cheyne-Stokes resp. Airway seems obst. Suctioned thick mucous. Cont. Cyanotic BP 87/44. P 165 irreg.

2:45 AM   Restless. Struggling to breathe. P weak, irreg., diff. to count. BP 60/30. Suctioned thick mucous with no change in resp. Or breath

2:50 AM   Respiration improved, less restless.

3:00 AM   P 110, reg. BP 90/65 R 20

3:15 AM   Quiet. P 105 BP 100/70 R 20

3:30 AM   Quiet. Color imp. R reg 20

4:00 AM   Resting easy. BP 124/70 P 94

And so the notes continued until 7:00 AM when the private duty nurse went off and the regular floor nurses took over.

Milt continued to improve and by the end of the week he was ready to go home. He was breathing better than I had ever known him to breathe in the four or five years that I had cared for him.

I was in his room giving him and his wife some last minute instructions when Milt interrupted to say, "You know Doc, I never was much about going to church. I did once in a while, when I had to. And I've done a lot of things I ain't proud to admit. But something's happened to me and I want to tell you this: Come Easter Sunday [it was about two weeks away] I'm gonna walk up the steps of that church down the street from home. And another thing, you know those little glass balls with a mustard seed in them? It's got something to do with Faith. I'm going to get me one just to remind me. I ain't gonna ever forget the Voice that spoke to me."

It so happened that I had a mustard seed that I wore on a key chain. I took it off and gave it to Milt.

Milt did indeed walk into Church that Easter morning, and continued to do so after I moved to Richmond. Finally The Voice spoke once more. I expect it said, "It's time, Milt."

[It has been nearly forty years since this event took place, and I am writing it from memory. The times may not be exact, and the numbers for the vital signs are only similar to what I recall. My writing of the Nurses Notes are not as crisp and precise as only an RN can write them, but the fact that something happened to Milton Shumaker that night is very real. I will not attempt to explain it. I am certain that there are skeptics who may read this and say that I am exaggerating. I am not.

I sincerely believe that a physician who says that he does not believe in God has not practiced medicine for even a day.]

≈ ≈

8

LIFE BEGINS WITH A SHOESTRING
TIED IN A BOW

The telephone rang early on New Year's Day. Actually it wasn't early, it just seemed so. The voice on the other end of the line was unfamiliar; so was the name, Lawrence Blake.

"Mr. Banks [I had long since ceased to bristle at not being reverently referred to as Doctor], this is Lawrence Blake out at Flat Top," he began in a plaintive voice. "We've never had you to doctor us but I was wondering if I could get you to come out to see my wife."

"Tell me what you think the trouble is, Mr. Blake," I asked. The snow was deep and I didn't relish going to Flat Top where the elevation was almost a thousand feet higher, and was one of the places where winter had been invented.

"Well, she had a baby last night. The snow was so bad I didn't want you coming out in it, so I delivered him myself. I just thought maybe you better check her and him to see if everything is all right."

"She hadn't seen a doctor about her pregnancy?"

"No. We hadn't seen no one. She's had babies before, and we was just going to wait until her time and call you. We just didn't think about it might snow."

I was impressed by his sincerity. I got directions to his house and promised that I would be out.

The highway had been cleared. The side road out to the Blakes' farm had not.

The Blakes lived in a remote corner of the county. The narrow road leading to their place was untracked by other vehicles, but a trail of footprints had shuffled through the eight or ten inches of snow to and from the last house I had passed, two miles back. Mr. Blake's trek to a telephone, I guessed.

The house was perched on a ridge that looked out over a countless stream of valleys and other ridges, and faded into the white oblivion of a pristine winterscape. Mr. Blake appeared on the porch of the neat, but sparse, two-storied house before I could even turn off the ignition.

He was a small man with a wide grin and one eye that strayed off to the side, unseeing and whitened from previous injury. He was full of apologies for having to call me out in such weather. He had shoveled a path from the porch to the gate.

Mrs. Blake was lying in a brass bed in the parlor. The room was comfortably heated by a "Warm Morning" stove, and a good supply of firewood stood nearby. Several children, all neatly dressed and combed, were lined up on the couch. They stood up as I entered the room and Mr. Blake introduced each of them. "Now go in the kitchen while Mr. Banks checks your mother and little brother."

Mrs. Blake appeared to be slightly taller than her husband, and considerably heavier. She smiled proudly as she turned back the covers to expose the new baby lying beside her, pink and pudgy, and sleeping contentedly against her bosom.

She was fine. Normal blood pressure, no fever, uterus well contracted, and very little postpartum bleeding. The baby weighed nearly nine pounds, but the hand-held scales carried in my OB

Bag were not supposed to give much more than a general idea and, since most every physician that did home deliveries used a similar scale, the average birth weight in that period appeared to be much better than it really was.

The baby was fine. The umbilical cord had been tied with a shoestring.

"I just took a string out of the white shoes one of the little girls had for church, washed it and boiled it, and used it to tie the cord," Lawrence said, proudly. The extent of his pride in his accomplishment was obvious by the tone of his voice. It was also obvious on the baby. The shoestring about the stub of the umbilical cord was tied in a neat, perky bow.

~

The most profound advice about obstetrics is that the doctor should assume an attitude of "Watchful Expectancy." For some reason, as far as the Blake family was concerned, I had a difficult time following that dictum.

It was fall, a beautiful day with a cerulean sky, and an Indian Summer crispness was grasping at the edge of the afternoon. Mrs. Blake was in labor, which was difficult to believe when you looked at her gentle smile as she laid propped up in bed and knitted away at booties for the new member of the Blake family. The booties were a generic blue/pink to fit any eventuality.

In the not too far distance could be heard the pop of shotguns as others more fortunate than I enjoyed the beginning of squirrel season. I was envious as I sat there on the porch with Lawrence.

Lawrence volunteered the information that there were several squirrels in the woodlot just a few hundred feet from the house and, if I thought that there was time, I could probably walk over there and get a mess, if I had the mind to.

"I can watch things here, and it ain't but a step over there, and I could call you in time to get back," he said.

I mulled it over for a while. I checked Mrs. Blake, and her contractions were irregular and not protracted. She was only about four centimeters dilated and the membranes were intact. Lawrence's suggestion sounded better all the time. This was the first day of hunting season, and I had put my gun in the car that morning where it would remain until the first week in January.

I told Lawrence that I would just walk over there and look to see if there was any sign of squirrels' cutting.

Squirrels had been cutting all over the place. Hickory nut cuttings were thick. I sat down and waited.

Before long I heard the branches of a tree shake as a squirrel jumped from limb to limb. I had my finger on the safety and was waiting, oblivious to all except the rattle of leaves. From the distance a call floated over the autumn air, "Mr. Banks, Mr. Banks!"

By the time I reached the house the baby had arrived several minutes before. Lawrence was smiling broadly and was waiting for me to arrive so that I could have the pleasure of cutting and tying the cord.

"I'm sorry I interrupted your hunt," Mrs. Blake said, and the expression on her face was sincere. "My water broke and this baby was here before I could even call Lawrence."

Our association continued on through house calls, and office visits, for minor ailments. Every Easter Lawrence would appear with a couple of dozen white eggs, washed and shined, and ready for dyeing. "White eggs is far the best for Easter Eggs," he would say.

I was beginning to think that the Blakes were practicing strict birth control, because it had been three years since I had missed delivering their last baby. Then Mrs. Blake appeared in the office, pregnant once again. She did well in her pregnancy.

Lawrence called me in the middle of the night. "Mr. Banks, I hate to wake you up," he said in his usual plaintive voice, "but my wife said she thought I ought to call you. Her pains have started and she says they is harder then any she's ever had."

I went immediately. If she was complaining, it had to be something out of the ordinary.

She was in hard labor when I arrived, and the cervix was almost completely dilated. The baby's head, however, was not descending as it should. I was suspicious that the head was posterior. Yet the baby did not seem to be stressed, judging by the heart rate. My main concern was the anxiety that Mrs. Blake was experiencing. It was so out of character. We sat through the night, waiting. Finally it was daylight and still she labored. The head was descending ever so slowly through a birth canal that had passed seven children without difficulty. The baby had descended enough that I could be certain that it was an occiput-posterior. Lawrence was getting nervous over this unusual situation. "Do you think we ought to take her into the hospital, Mr. Banks?"

I had been considering that option myself. The baby's heart rate was increasing.

The only transportation available was my Jeep station wagon. Together we got her into the back of the station wagon, on a pad of several blankets and a quilt, and started for the hospital twelve miles away. We were about three miles down the road when Mrs. Blake yelled, "It's coming! It's coming!"

I pulled over and slammed on the brakes, jumped out, and ran around and opened the back of the station wagon. The membranes had ruptured and the head was beginning to crown. It was an occiput-posterior as I had determined. The baby was coming out face-up, and it was a big baby.

I stood there on the side of the road and delivered the baby, cut and tied the cord, delivered the placenta and checked the mother. She had a small perineal tear which I would repair when I got her back home. During the entire episode, a School Bus was waiting patiently to get out of the side road and proceed on its mission to deliver the students for the first day of school. The students were crowded up in the front of the bus witnessing what had to be the most bizarre beginning of a first day of school. I have often wondered if they were late, and if so, what did they tell their teachers. And moreover, did the teachers believe them?

Mrs. Blake was overjoyed that the baby had come out "looking up," as she put it. "They say babies that come out 'looking up' are almost sure to be preachers," she said.

When I filled out the birth certificate, in the space that asked where the baby was born, I was tempted to write, "At the junction of the road to Ellison and US 19."

Watchful expectancy? It seemed that no matter how much, or how hard I watched, with Mrs. Blake it was always unexpected.

≈ ≈

9

THE MUD OF WINTER

Blue Jay 6 was remote. I have never really known how its name came about. I suppose it had to do with the site of a lumber camp from the old Blue Jay Lumber Company. It wasn't really a town or village, it was more correctly an area. I enjoyed going into Blue Jay 6, mostly because it was so remote.

Ralph and his family were among the patients that I saw there. They lived up a rutted lane about a half-mile from the road, which in itself deserved some imagination to be awarded that term. At the end of the lane that passed through a heavily timbered area, the land opened into a lovely cove of small pastures and meadows, graced by a nice bungalow and several well-kept outbuildings. Getting there in summer was easy. The first time I went there, it was winter.

I parked my Buick Special on the side of the road and looked doubtfully at the lane. It was first class mud. Ralph had said so when he called. I had thought he was exaggerating; now I could see that he had understated the situation.

I pulled on some rubber overshoes and began walking the half-mile or so to the house, trying to stay in the middle of the lane, and to walk on the frozen stretches as much as possible. The sun was just beginning to make itself known, filtering its rays down through the bare branches of the trees at nearly noon of a late February day.

Ralph's wife had the flu. So did most everybody else in the county. I did what I could, which was mostly taking her temperature, looking at her throat, and listening to her chest. Some aspirin and some instructions completed my call. Then I had to stay to lunch, or dinner as it really was, prepared by the patient's mother who had come to care for her daughter during her illness. The food was excellent, and Ralph and I visited over coffee and cherry pie, the cherries having been canned from the crop of several trees that graced the perimeter of the yard. I really had wasted too much time. There were other calls to make.

Ralph promised to call me again if his wife wasn't greatly improved in the next couple of days, and I started back down the lane to my car.

The sun had done its job on the lane. What had been muddy ruts was now total quagmire. The frozen middle of the lane no longer existed. To walk in the woods was to walk in a foot or so of wet snow, and through thick briers. I slogged onward, my feet soaking wet, mud well over my ankles and sloshing about in my shoes. At times I wondered if I was going to be able to pull my feet free from the mud. Toward the end there was so much mud in my shoes that it felt as if I was actually barefoot.

At last the car was in view. I reached out to touch it with a grateful hand, and then leaned against it to remove my overshoes. There were no overshoes. Also there was no left shoe. They were all somewhere in Ralph's lane.

The next day I bought a Jeep Station Wagon.

~

One good thing about house calls at Blue Jay 6 was the hunting. During the hunting season I kept my shotgun in the car, along with some coveralls and some boots. If I passed some likely cover, and had the time, I would stop and hunt for a few minutes.

The grouse were plentiful and it wasn't difficult to flush one or two in thirty minutes or so of hunting.

There was one particularly good looking field, heavily grown up in ragweed, that had a long stretch of haws bushes, laced with greenbriers, that filled a swale in the field for its entire width, up to the woods. A couple of volunteer apple trees were interspersed in the thicket. It spelled grouse.

I had a few minutes one evening and stopped to try walking up through the thicket. I put on my coveralls and boots and eased over into the field. Before approaching the thicket, I decided that I would be more comfortable if I relieved myself first. I put my gun down to do so, and within moments a grouse thundered out of the thicket, straight away up the field. It was a big bird, a male with a broad fan. That was the only grouse in the thicket.

Several days later I took a "short-cut" past the field. It was only a few miles out of the way. I got into the coveralls and boots, slipped a couple of shells in the Ithaca double, and started into the field and its thicket.

I walked slowly up the right side of the thicket, pausing frequently, and waiting expectantly. I heard the grouse flush on the far side of the thicket, but he was a good sixty yards away when he came up into view. I would almost swear that I saw him flick his tail in derision.

I tried it again the following week. This time I went up the left side. The grouse rolled out on the right side, well hidden until he was out of range.

It was the last day of the season before I could get there again. I had hunted another spot first and had taken a couple of birds, but I wanted to give my old friend another try.

"This time, you old devil, I'm coming up the middle, I'm going to be ready, and the moment you flush, I'm going to bust you with some size 7 shot," I said aloud, almost expecting him to hear and understand my threat. This bird had really gotten to me.

I entered the thicket and began pushing my way through the haws and the greenbriers. It was rough going and it hurt. Periodically I would pause and wait, the silence broken only by my breathing from the exertion of fighting the thicket.

I was nearly halfway to the woods when the bird flushed. He went almost straight up for about ten feet and then leveled off, straight away up the middle of the thicket, a wide open shot.

The Ithaca was tight against my shoulder, the image of the going away bird was sitting right on top of the barrel, when I saw him flick his tail again. I watched over the barrel as he sailed up the thicket and, just as he went into the woods, I yelled, "Bang!"

I hoped he heard me.

~

It was a bright, sunny morning. The snow was gone, except for a few piles from shoveling, and some drifts. Winter was over and we could look forward to spring. I was just finishing breakfast when an item near the bottom of the page of the morning paper caught my eye. It mentioned the name of my old friend Ralph; he had been arrested for making whiskey.

Later in the day, Ralph walked into the office.

"The paper said you were in jail," I said.

"I was. They let me out today. I stopped by here on the way home so as I could get something for my nerves."

Then he began his sad story.

"Well, I got the flu after you was up to see my wife. There was so much snow and mud and stuff that I didn't want you to have to come out there. Besides, I'd heard you tell her what to do, and we still had some of them pills, so I just took them and stayed quiet like you said, and drunk a lot of water and some hot toddies. It got real warm this week, you know, and I was a-lying out on the porch. I was too weak to do much else. It was just so pretty that I thought I would fire up the still. I had some mash that had been workin' for a pretty good spell. So I go out and fire things up. It was just beginning to run good when here they come a-swoopin' down on me."

Ralph paused, and stood there shaking his head, reliving the ordeal.

"The worst thing," he continued, "was they took axes and chopped holes in my boiler and cut up the coil in little bitty pieces. That was my granddaddy's still, maybe even his daddy's. And the worst part was, I had to stand there and watch 'em do it." He brushed some moisture from his eyes. "My nerves is just shot all to hell, Doc."

10

"NOR WILL I PRESCRIBE A DEADLY DRUG"
(Hippocrates)

The lady sitting across from me was tall, attractive, well groomed, and articulate. She was home from New York where she had lived for a number of years. Her brother was well known to me and for that reason she had come to my office. Her main complaint was abdominal pain. A spastic colon, a doctor in New York had told her about a year ago.

She didn't look like a spastic colon; her complexion was sallow, and there was too much loose skin around her neck, as if she had lost weight. Yes, she had lost weight, she said in response to my question. And yes, she felt tired most of the time, and her abdomen hurt, and she was spotting blood.

The question was answered by pelvic examination. She had a far advanced carcinoma of the cervix. The vaginal walls were plastered down by the extension of the cancer into the pelvis. On rectal exam the same masses could be felt.

I referred her to a Gynecologist who referred her to a Medical Center in another state where she was operated upon, received radiation, and was sent home to die.

She was staying with her brother, not far from my office, and I would stop by every few days to visit and to make sure that there was plenty of morphine that her brother and sister-in-law were giving for her pain. It was heart-rending to watch her melting away as the relentless cancer gnawed at her body. It was already taking its toll when I first saw her. Now, just months later, it was difficult to imagine how such loveliness could be destroyed in such a short time.

The phone rang just before I left the office one night. It was her brother asking if I could stop by the house for a minute. Of course I could.

She had deteriorated even more since I had seen her just a few days before. She was getting her morphine every two hours and it was not enough. A quarter of a grain made the pain bearable for a few minutes, but then it was agony until time for the next dose.

Her brother and his wife sat there beside the bed as we talked.

She asked, "Doctor, how much longer will this go on?"

I told her I didn't know.

She said, "What would happen if you gave me some of that in a vein?" and she nodded toward the vial of morphine. "A lot of it?"

I said that she would die.

"Would you?" she asked. "Please?"

I didn't answer for a moment. I struggled with my conscience. I wanted to answer yes so badly, but I was young and I thought that doctors only tried to save lives, prolong life. We also felt that we alleviated suffering, but paradoxically we often extended it, just as I was doing. Her pleading eyes were fixed on mine. Finally I said that I could not do that, even as badly as I wanted to. Her "Please!" was tearing me apart.

Her brother helped. "We understand," he said.

As I was leaving she took my hand in both of hers and held it against her cheek. "Thank you, thank you for everything."

She didn't say good-bye, but I really knew that she meant it.

Bessie asked, as I walked in the office the next morning, if I had heard that she had died during the night. I said that I had not heard the news.

But I knew.

☙11☙

PLACEBOES, MEDDLING AND FISHHOOKS

A placebo is a medication given to satisfy a patient's wish for medicine, or the attention that accompanies the medication. It has absolutely no value in the treatment of the medical problem. Sometimes it can be very successful for the immediate problem. At times it can produce problems, as it did in this case.

The woman was lying on the bed, twitching slightly, her eyes closed, but the lids could be seen to flutter ever so faintly if you looked closely. A few minutes before she had been in a full-blown convulsive seizure, thrashing about on the bed and bouncing dangerously close to the edge. I sat and watched.

"Catch her before she falls off of the bed," a neighbor woman had yelled.

It wasn't necessary to catch her. Forewarned, she immediately began thrashing and bouncing back to the middle of the bed.

I gave her an injection of saline and the seizure stopped. Now she was "sleeping" peacefully from her dose of medication. Except her eyelids fluttered if you watched closely.

It wasn't many days before I was back there again. Another convulsive seizure. Once again 1 cc of saline took care of the problem.

It seemed that she attributed her problem to having a back operation for a ruptured disc a few years before. I couldn't elicit any signs of recurrent disc problems. She, on the other hand, had decided that somehow a bunch of nerves had grown together, and when she did certain things, such as housework, cooking, laundry, and other wifely chores–and she stressed the "wifely chores"–she had a seizure. The seizures only occurred when her husband was home, and he traveled a lot. I had never been called there otherwise.

I had tried to suggest that it might be a good idea to consult a Psychiatrist without coming right out and saying this woman had a serious problem. In those days people were not quite so prone to accept psychiatric problems. To suggest such was the same as saying a patient was crazy, and that meant going to the State Hospital for the Insane and never coming back. But I was also feeling guilty over the fact that I was charging this man $5.00 for coming out to his house every few days for this.

Finally, after a full-blown seizure in which the saline had its usual instantaneous effect, I was walking to my Jeep, the husband going along with me.

"Doc, just what's wrong with the old lady, anyhow?" he asked. "Ain't she ever gonna get better?"

"Frankly, I don't think there is anything wrong except her head. She needs a Psychiatrist. I haven't given her anything except an injection of saline, salt water, and she stops her convulsion each time. It's all in her head," I said.

He looked at me for a long moment, and then grinned.

"Thanks, Doc. Thanks a lot." His handshake was strong.

It was about two weeks later when he walked into the office with a package.

"Here's some T-bone steaks for you Doc. I just slaughtered a steer. Thought you might like these. You remember that last time when you were out to the house, and said there wasn't anything wrong with the old lady except her head? Well sir, after you left I went back in the house and said, 'Get your lazy butt out of bed and fix me some supper.' She got up, packed a suitcase and left, and I ain't seen her since."

~

Doctors can be very opinionated, especially when something crosses the line drawn by science.

I was checking the elderly lady's leg because of her complaint of swelling. She had some varicose veins but little else of note. Her leg was not painful and there was no evidence of thrombophlebitis, the inflammation that produces blood clots in the veins. The swelling was worse at the end of the day and was most likely due to the poor venous return associated with the varicosities.

In the course of examination I noticed a piece of red yarn tied about her fifth toe. It had obviously been in place a long time.

"What's this for," I asked.

"It's to keep my corn from getting red and sore," she answered. "I've been wearing it a long time. When one wears out, I tie on a new one."

The yarn wasn't tight, it was not obstructing circulation, it wasn't doing anything, and certainly not any harm.

"Rubbish," I said, and snipped off the piece of yarn.

The lady looked at me knowingly, and with a sneer said, "You don't know everything. My toe's going to get red and sore, just you wait and see."

Four days later, with the office full of patients, she walked into the office and sat down in the waiting room. She removed her shoe and stocking and told Bessie, "Tell that doctor to come out here and look at this."

I walked into the room. She had her foot propped up on a chair for all the world to see, and it seemed that most of the world was sitting there. The fifth toe was swollen to at least three times its normal size, and horribly inflamed.

The old lady glared at me, "See that? I told you what would happen when you cut that yarn off of my toe."

The other patients in the room snickered. She put on her stocking and shoe and limped out of the office. I never saw her again.

Moral: Don't meddle with something you don't know about. Doctors don't know everything.

~

Ed Kincaid called one Sunday morning to say that a man was down at the office with a fishhook caught in his lip.

When I drove up, the man was sitting on the porch, leaning against one of the posts, asleep. A large hook had gone completely through the upper lip on the left side. A piece of the catgut snell hung down over the side of his mouth, along with a large, dried out and shriveled up, night crawler that was pushed up on the shank of the hook.

I got the man on his feet and into the office.

"How did you do this?"

"I ain't real sure, Doc. We was trotlining down on the river, and I was takin' this big ol' catfish off, and somehow he flopped and made the next

65

hook come up and get me. At least I guess that was it."

During this speech he would pause periodically and blow the dried worm out of the way, and from the smell of his breath it was obvious why the events of the night were not entirely clear in his mind.

"What time did all this happen," I asked. "Oh, I guess long about two, maybe two-thirty. I didn't want to bother you in the night time, so we just went on fishing."

By that time I had removed the worm and cut the barb off and removed the hook. After I had cleaned the wound and given him a tetanus booster, I just had to ask, "Why didn't you at least take the worm off of the hook?"

"Didn't think about it I guess. Because of the hook, I had to drink out of the right side of my mouth, so I never noticed it, much."

He paid me with a big catfish.

≈ ≋

☞12☜

DOCTORS HAVE IT EASY NOW

I was mumbling to myself about the trials of being a country doctor, having to make house calls in the middle of the night, in all kinds of weather, and how this particular night wasn't fit for man nor beast, what with the snow and cold, and it being after midnight. I had driven six or eight miles in my Jeep station wagon with the heater going full blast. It was a rough life, I thought.

I drove up to the house and the porch light was burning as an indicator that I had reached my destination. The man met me at the door, much too jovial for that hour of the night, his good mood wasted on a person in such a foul humor as I.

I bristled at his greeting, "You young doctors sure have it easy," he said. Before I could take issue with the statement, he continued, "I remember a night just like this, about the same time of year, that your Dad rode out here on horseback to see my mother. She had pneumonia. He stayed right here for almost two days, doing everything he could until she died. He slept on that couch right over there," and he pointed to a stout, black leather couch that didn't look very comfortable for sitting, or sleeping.

The man's wife also had pneumonia. I treated her with antibiotics, never being aware of having much concern that she wouldn't recover, never considering that it might be necessary for me to spend the night, or a few days, waiting for "the crisis," that dreaded time in the course of an infectious disease which would indicate that a patient would or would

67

not recover. It was especially dramatic in the course of lobar pneumonia.

I thought about this on the way home. I was warm and dry. The visit had taken less than an hour, counting travel time. My father had once made the same trip by horseback, probably at least an hour's ride, and there are few places that a person can be colder than on a horse's back. He had to stay and watch the patient die, undoubtedly working with cold compresses to reduce fever, medications to relieve pain, other medications to make breathing easier, and knowing that the final outcome was beyond his hands. I had no doubt that my patient would be much improved the following day.

It was an excellent lesson in humility.

The man was right. Doctors have it easy now.

⮰13⮰

THE CHRISTMAS TREE

It was the Christmas Season. My Jeep was loaded with several boxes of groceries, including a turkey. There were also gaily wrapped presents, suitable for a mixture of children of varying ages. Gloves, scarves, hats, a few toys, and other things that would bring happiness. I was delivering it for the Presbyterian Church in Beckley.

In the road ahead of me I could see the children for whom the gifts were intended, walking homeward. I stopped and offered them a ride. They recognized my vehicle, and they knew that my destination must be their house for there was no other house on the road.

They were returning from school, and the day had ended with a Christmas party. Each of them had a small gift that they held tightly in their hands, having rewrapped them in the white tissue paper. Every now and then they would slip a piece of hard candy into their mouths. One of them offered me a small, brown bag to choose a piece. They were happy, and the oldest child began singing Jingle Bells. We all joined in.

They gave shy, inquisitive glances at the boxes behind the seat but made no mention of the contents, even though the legs of the turkey were quite obvious.

The house was built of logs. It sat on the edge of the mountain that looked over the Bluestone gorge, and beyond it, into a wilderness shrouded by snow mingling with the fog. There was a homemade sled neatly stored away out of the weather, beneath the porch of the cabin, and I thought of the times that I had picked up my children's sleds out of the driveway.

Their mother came out to meet us. She was middle-aged, not so much for how long she had lived, but mostly from how she had lived. Her face was flushed from the stove in which she had a cake baking. Her hands were red and chapped from the constant exposure of dipping and carrying water from the spring. Her abdomen was already enlarged from the baby that would be born in the spring. Her oldest daughter had presented her with a grandchild that I had delivered the previous summer. Her oldest son was in the service. The other four were climbing out of my car.

I explained to her that the boxes that I was delivering were from the Presbyterian Church. She smiled gratefully, and she and the children helped me carry them into the house.

"Come in and see our Christmas Tree," the youngest girl urged, taking me by the hand and leading me into the main room.

Standing before the window was a small white pine, about five feet tall. It was wrapped with chains made in school from colored construction paper. There were several red and green paper discs, cut from the fronts of Lucky Strike cigarette packs, and pierced with string to suspend them from the tree boughs. From the top of the tree hung a solitary, red, glass ball, the only purchased ornament on the tree.

Each of the children carefully placed the gifts that they had received at school underneath the tree and stood back to admire it.

"Isn't it pretty?" the little girl said, looking up at me with bright, excited eyes, jerking on my hand with both of hers, as if she had to pump an answer from me.

"It's the prettiest Christmas tree I have ever seen," I told her, truthfully.

The husband was away. He had gotten some work that day. She said he would be sorry that he missed me. She offered me a cup of coffee and we visited for a few minutes. The children took the homemade sled from beneath the porch and began taking turns sliding down the road that had led us to the house.

When I left, she thanked me again and asked that I thank the church for them. It was going to be such a nice Christmas for the children, and they had so much to be grateful for. As I got in the Jeep she called out, "I'll be into the office for my visit as soon as the weather permits."

When the weather permitted, she and her husband were killed in a head-on collision, not far from my office.

A few days after the funeral, the grown daughter came in to talk about the situation. She didn't feel that she was in a position that she could raise her younger siblings. Her oldest brother was in the Army, and she didn't know what she could do. Did I have any suggestions?

I called a friend who had some connection with a Presbyterian Home/School, and he was able to get the children admitted there.

Sometime later a State Trooper friend came to me and said that he had heard that the older brother was home on leave from the service, and he was pretty upset that I had had the children placed in an "Orphanage" and he was looking for me, and what he had in mind didn't sound very pleasant. The trooper said if I had any trouble to let him know. The only problem was, from what I had been told, there wasn't going to be time to let the trooper know.

I never heard any more about it; the children remained at the school, graduated, and are now successful citizens. I checked with the school not long ago and was told that they had returned for a reunion there a few years ago.

For a while however, I was feeling as if I had meddled once too often.

≈   ∽

❧14❧

THE SERVICE STATION

The hospital called one late summer evening and said that one of my patients was there and had been bitten by a copperhead.

The bite was on his thumb and it was slightly swollen. He didn't want any treatment for himself. He wanted some antivenom to take home for his coon hound.

He had been down on Glade Creek with his dog, "Runnin' him to git him into shape," he explained, "when I seen him fightin' this ol' copperhead. I seen a stick out'ten the corner of my eye and I retched down to git it when, Wham!, that damn stick bit me. It was another damn copperhead. But we killed 'em both."

The dog had been bitten about the face and he was quite concerned about him, so he carried the dog up the mountain to his house, and then walked some distance to a neighbor's to get him to bring him to the hospital for something for his dog.

"He's the best coon dog in the county, Doc."

I assured him that it would be very unlikely for a copperhead bite to do much to a big hound, and for further assurance, I called a Veterinarian friend who agreed. "Just keep him quiet, his head will swell some, but he'll do fine," I told him.

By that time his arm was beginning to swell. I gave him some antivenom and, over his objection, admitted him overnight for observation. Despite a negative skin test before receiving the antivenom, the next morning he had the worst case of hives I have

73

ever seen. Why I thought he would be more suscep-tible to the snake bite than his hound, is a mystery to me now.

A few days later, at the Beaver Service Station, the local philosophers were discussing the case. One of them said that it wasn't necessary to kill the snake that had bitten the man, it would have died anyway.

More knowledge (some of very questionable value), and more lies, passed through the Beaver Service Station than any place in the county. Every morning and every afternoon, a group would gather to discuss whatever topic was big in the news at the moment. One thing would lead to another so fast that it was difficult to separate current events from out and out lies. This was especially true in regard to fishing and hunting.

Walter began a tale one fall day, when the dis-cussion had gotten around to hunting. It seemed that he had been riding along in the truck with Tracy, who had some groceries to deliver.

"I seen this pheasant [many of the older locals called grouse, pheasants] fly across in front of me and Tracy, and it flew into a power line. I yelled at Tracy to stop, and I run back there and picked it up. That pheasant's head was tore clean off! I threw it in the back of the truck and took it home. That night I cleaned it, and you know there wasn't a mark on that bird. I just threw it away."

"Why'd you throw it away, Walter?" some-body asked.

"Heck, I wasn't gonna take no chances. It's no tellin what that bird might have died from."

"Don't you think cutting his head off on a wire is a good enough reason?"

"Well maybe, but you can't be too careful these days," Walter replied.

~

Another time the talk had turned to strength. Walter said it was true that if you lifted a calf over a fence every day from the day it was born, when it got to be a full grown steer, you could still lift it over the fence. He said, "I knowed a man down on Little Bluestone that did it, and that's the gospel truth, and I can prove it. I'll just take you down there and show you the fence he lifted it over."

~

One of the most revolting things that ever happened, happened to Walter. He had the bad habit of moving about the station, and any Coca Cola bottle that didn't have a protective hand on it was most likely going to be finished by Walter, in one or two gulps.

Andy chewed tobacco, and he would wander into the station and pick an empty bottle out of the rack and use it to deposit his tobacco juice. That does make you a little uneasy about returnable bottles.

Somebody took one of those bottles, added a little soda to it, recapped it and stuck it back in a corner of the chest-type cooler. A few days later Walter was seen coming down the road. The half-full bottle was taken from the cooler, the cap was removed and the bottle placed on the counter, unattended. The conversation went on as usual.

Walter walked in, spoke to everybody, and listened to the conversation while glancing about the room for a Coca Cola that was unattended. He spotted the bottle and eased around the room until he was leaning against the counter. He cautiously extended his hand to the cold bottle. In a flash he had turned the bottle up and drained the contents in two swallows. He didn't say a word, or make even a sound. He just walked out of the station and down the road.

Walter never mentioned it. It was a long time before any of those involved could talk about it. It was a long time before Walter ever touched another Coca Cola bottle.

≈15≈

". . . FILLED WITH THE ENDS OF WORMS"
(The Hobbit)

The boy was about six. He was pale and his abdomen was distended and tight. The bowel sounds were rumbling around in his belly like a volcano ready to erupt. His abdomen wasn't tender, he had no fever, he hadn't been nauseated, he was just bloated and uncomfortable.

His siblings crowded around the bed, their curiosity frequently pushing them closer to the bed than I was. As I finished my examination, one of them reached out and pushed on the distended abdomen with a dirt-coated finger, drew it back, and shook his head sadly.

"Do you have an enema bag," I asked the mother.

"A what?"

I didn't think I was going to get very far with this approach.

"A syringe? A douche bag? Something we can use to give this boy an enema . . . wash his bowels out," I said.

She finally understood and produced a fairly large bulb syringe, some warm water and some soap. I proceeded to give the child an enema. The siblings giggled.

"You kids git outside. Git now, or you'll be next," the mother yelled. They scattered like baby quail, and then stood outside the room looking in. The giggling had stopped.

Since the house had no plumbing, and there was no way to get the child to the outhouse, I instructed the mother to bring a chamber pot to the bedside. She didn't have one of those. A bucket maybe? Or anything, and quick, this kid was about to erupt.

She brought a coffee can. I had my doubts that it was going to be big enough but there wasn't time to argue the point; Vesuvius was about to blow.

The little boy jumped up and squatted down over the can. A ball of round worms, as big as a softball, plopped out into the can. It filled the can and spilled out on the floor. Worms went everywhere, swimming happily along in the soapy water that was trickling across the uneven floor. The gas followed in the same fluttering, whistling fashion as a balloon does when the air is suddenly released.

"Lawsey me," the mother exclaimed.

The siblings were nowhere to be seen.

The little boy climbed back on the bed. Tears of fear and embarrassment had carved little furrows down his grimy cheeks. He felt gently at first, and then ran his hands over his now flat belly. He smiled the snaggle-toothed smile of a six year old.

"That sure was a good fart," he said proudly.

≈ ≈

≈16≈

TO MEDDLE OR NOT TO MEDDLE

The little girl was the classical, clinical picture of scarlet fever: sore throat, chills, fever, the diffuse rash that blanched with pressure, and the "strawberry tongue" that is produced by the swollen papillae (taste buds) protruding through the bright red coating of the tongue, and especially the circumoral pallor that is so characteristic of the disease.

The child was about ten years of age and lived with her mother, older sister, and brother. The husband/father was a career army man and overseas.

Penicillin injections for her infection caused me to stop by daily. The visits became even more necessary when her blood pressure began going up and she developed other signs of acute glomerulonephritis.

Fortunately she responded to treatment. Her blood pressure returned to normal, and the urine no longer showed evidence of proteinuria and the blood and casts, the microscopic evidence of the urine of glomerulonephritis. But over the weeks of treatment the family had become very special, as is the case so many times in Family Practice. A couple of years later the mother appeared in my office, very distraught over a letter she had received from her husband, and she had me read the letter.

He was stationed in Europe. In his letter he explained how, in his loneliness, he had met a young lady; they became friendly, and, shamefully and apologetically, he admitted to giving into other urges, as a result of which the lady had become pregnant. Because of the laws of that nation in which he was stationed, he would have to marry the lady, and so must divorce his wife, but only for a while. He would marry the lady, and when the baby was born and had a proper, legal name, he would divorce that wife and return to his American family.

"What can I do," the heart-broken wife cried.

I told her that I would try to get some advice about this problem.

I called a young attorney friend about the problem and went up to his office to discuss it. He said that if there was some way to get the man back to this country, then the laws of the European country would not apply, and he doubted that such a problem would lead to extradition.

The family of the wife had a long history of coronary disease. In fact, two of her brothers had died of heart attacks, one fairly recently. So I devised the plan of her having a "heart attack." We would get hold of the Red Cross and have her husband brought back to the United States, and everything would be coming up roses.

So we did. She called me and complained of chest pains, I went down to her house and was somewhat shocked at the sight of her; pale, sweating, weakness, and pain. If she was acting, she was doing an excellent job of it. I called an ambulance and had her taken to the hospital. There was no evidence of a coronary, but the Red Cross was called and within a few days the husband was home. By the time he got here she had recovered from what was diagnosed as an acute esophagitis from a hiatal hernia that had been demonstrated on X-ray.

Within a week she was as good as new. That was when her husband appeared in the office.

"Doc," he began, "just how serious is my wife's problem?"

I explained that she had a hiatal hernia. It was nothing serious at this time, and she had not had a heart attack as we had first thought.

"Then it will be okay for me to go back to my outfit in Europe?" he asked.

There was nothing left but to explain to him just what had transpired: that his wife had confided in me about the situation in Europe, and we had planned a "heart attack" to get him home. The esophagitis attack had just been icing on the cake at an opportune time.

"Hell, Doc, I was just trying to let my wife down easy. I just made up that stuff about the girl being pregnant. I really want a divorce so I can marry her."

He went back to Europe. I left shortly thereafter to take a residency in Orthopaedic Surgery, so I lost out on other episodes of the saga.

Once again, the moral is, "don't meddle." It seemed a hard lesson for me to learn.

≈ ∽

≈17≈

CHASTITY CAN CAUSE PROBLEMS TOO

Hymen was the god of marriage in Greek mythology. Hymen is also an anatomical structure consisting of a fold of mucous membrane at the vaginal orifice and supposedly signifies virginity. If what we read in various magazines, newspapers, and periodicals of questionable value is true, the significance of a hymen is becoming rare indeed. There was a time however that a hymen came in many shapes, sizes and forms, and sometimes presented a lot more problems than just as an indicator of chastity.

The girl was young and pretty, bright and alert, popular and smart. The fact that she was precocious in her development escaped the adults that surrounded her. It also escaped notice by several physicians, including me.

My first contact with the problem came when she was seen for acute abdominal pain, associated with tenderness in the right lower quadrant. I referred her to a surgeon who examined her and kept her overnight for observation. When the pain cleared up and there were no further problems, he sent her home. In retrospect, this was probably what is referred to as Mittelschmerz, pain caused by minor bleeding when the ovum, the egg, breaks out of its follicle on the ovary, except nobody thought of it at the time.

A few months later there was another episode of pain and tenderness and once again the same scenario of referral and observation.

It happened with fair regularity for over a year. The mother became so inured to the problem that she would put the child to bed with an ice pack, which afforded relief. We were also oblivious to the fact that this child often didn't "feel good." Finally there was one occasion when the pain continued and the mother arrived in the office with the girl in extreme pain.

On examination there was no question that something was going on in the abdomen. A mass was easily palpable, firm and tender to pressure just above the pubis.

I explained to the girl, and to her mother, that I was going to do a rectal examination to see what this mass was. The rectal exam was not necessary. It became evident when she turned on her side and drew up her legs, and a dark, bulging mass was seen at the vaginal orifice. She had an imperforate hymen, one that completely occluded the vaginal orifice. She had begun menstruating, and each month the bleeding collected in the vagina until finally it became so distended that the uterus was easily palpable above the pubis. Almost a quart of old blood was released when the hymen was divided. The girl was ten years old.

~

A young husband called me during the night and said that his wife was having a hemorrhage. I didn't put two and two together until I arrived at their little efficiency apartment and recognized them as newly-wed by only a few hours, and certainly this could not be a miscarriage as I had suspected when I was called.

The wedding had taken place in the late afternoon, and after the festivities of a small reception and supper, the bride and groom repaired to their little love nest where they were to spend their first night of wedded bliss. It was indeed a memorable wedding night.

The bride was sobbing, the groom was distraught, and together they were holding a blood soaked towel between her legs. The bed was a mass of blood.

They had come back to their apartment and prepared for bed, the groom in silk pajamas, the bride in a lacy gown and negligee, and all were soon discarded. Try as they might however, the union could not be made.

They would rest in each others arms until the heat of passion would once again urge them to try to consummate their marriage, but the pain the bride suffered would once again deter them.

Finally they decided that it could be done and it would be done! At last, penetration was achieved and was found to be less gratifying than either had anticipated; she because of pain and he because his compassion was stronger than his primal urge. They had both heard from their peers about "breaking the cherry," the giggling, school-ground explanation of rupturing the hymen with the first attempt at intercourse, and how some bleeding was to be expected. As a matter of fact, the usual explanation was bleeding had better happen or the girl was not a virgin, an untrue statement of course. There was certainly no question in this case. They both decided that this was much more than they had been led to expect. That was when the bride said her husband should call the doctor.

Examination revealed a very thick, tight, hymeneal ring that had torn through a small vessel that was still spurting a tiny stream of bright blood. The end of the vessel was easily seen, and I was able to grasp it with a hemostat and tie it off with a piece of catgut.

The still sobbing, anxious bride asked, "This won't happen every time will it?"

I assured her that it wouldn't.

The three of us removed the sheets and put them in cold water to soak and I left. The groom accompanied me to the car and asked how much he owed me. "Let's just call it a wedding present," I said. He smiled gratefully and then asked a favor. "You won't tell anybody about this will you?" Up until now I have kept that promise, and after forty odd years I doubt that it makes any difference.

≈ ≋

≈18≈

TAKE EACH STEP WITH CARE

He was a huge man. He lived up on the mountain above Beaver. We had hunted quail on his land forever it seemed. Each time we would stop to hunt, Dad always made it a point to stop at the house and tell him we were hunting. Most of the places we hunted, he just drove up, parked and started hunting. Not there. The man would acknowledge our presence, grin, and say, "Watch where you step."

It was years before I finally understood. He had a still, and he was cautioning us about its presence.

I inherited his family as patients, and also inherited the hunting privileges.

One day I was hunting with a good friend, and we stopped by there late in the afternoon. I told the man, and he said, "Watch where you step." I assured him that we would.

We found a covey of quail and took a couple apiece and left.

A few weeks later my friend stopped by the man's house and asked if it was okay to hunt, reminding him that he had been there with me. He said sure, and added his usual admonition about watching where he stepped. It was a bitter cold day, near Christmas, and as George started off into the field, the man called out to him, "When you finish, stop in the house and warm up."

George finished his hunt and came back to the house, put his German pointers, Rebel and Dixie, in the car and then knocked on the kitchen door and was admitted.

"I'm having a little drink, could I pour you one?"

George agreed and the man poured a water glass half full of moonshine.

They had a good visit and a couple more drinks of moonshine. George thought it was the best he had tasted. The man gave him a quart jar of it to take home.

He never remembered going home. His wife said that he dragged his coat and gun in the house, and collapsed on the bed. She decided he had had a heart attack and ran over to the neighbor to come and help. The neighbor said, "Hell, he's drunk and he's passed out."

George said it was two days before he could even walk, much less walk straight.

Several weeks later I saw the man's son at Charlie Anderson's Service Station. He said, "Daddy's still talking about that fellow you brought up there hunting, and how much he could drink. Daddy said he damn near out drunk him, and ain't many men can do that. What's that fellow do, anyhow?"

"He's an FBI agent," I said.

"Oh for God's sake, Daddy'll die when he hears that," the son said.

≈ ≈

≈19≈

PRIDE REVISITED

The little boy was the interpreter for me. He was signing to his parents who were both deaf mute. I was amazed to watch him and see what appeared to be the similarity of his signing to what is considered to be the level of language capability for a four year old. It looked like he was skipping over some parts of the language, much like very young children leave out certain adverbs, adjectives and prepositions from their speech, if that is possible in signing. Anyhow, we were getting the job done.

His mother was the patient, I can't remember exactly the problem, some upper respiratory ailment most likely, and it's not important. What is important is the pride that I felt for this very mature four year old. It happened this way.

I had just graduated from Medical School and was awaiting my orders to the U.S. Naval Hospital at Portsmouth, Va, for my internship. I was "sharing" my newly acquired knowledge of medicine with my father.

The call came into his office one morning that a young lady was in labor, one that he had agreed to care for at her time of delivery. I guess he told them that he would send me out to do the delivery, because he handed me his OB bag, told me how to get to the house, the patient's name, that she had done well in her pre-natal course, and no other details.

I had been on home deliveries before, with Dad and with my brother-in-law, so it was not something new for me. As a matter of fact, once during medical school, while I was on the OB service, and we were having a very busy night and all of the delivery rooms were full, the Chief of OB-Gyn was on the floor, and she decided to give us a demonstration of how to deliver a baby in the home, using a hospital bed on the ward as a "home." About the only comparison was that there was a bed involved. There any similarity to a home delivery ended.

The Chief was busy lecturing the students on the proper procedure to follow, lecturing with her back to the patient, when the baby popped out like someone spitting out a prune pit. So much for the professor's home delivery technique.

But off I went to deliver this baby. I found the house without a problem, and I was met at the door by a tall, angular lady. I told her who I was and that the senior Dr. Banks had sent me. She told me to come in. There were three or four women in the house, besides the patient. I was introduced to each of them in sign language. They were all deaf-mutes.

The lady who had come to the door was the oldest sister of the family. She could hear and speak. The mother, now quite elderly, was also able to hear and speak. All of the other children in the family had been born deaf-mutes, or whatever the present politically correct term is now. As each grew up, they went off to the West Virginia School for the Deaf, and each of them found a spouse with similar problems. They all lived in a small enclave in the same neighborhood, and got along very well. The sister and mother had both learned to sign, and more or less took care of the details that required voices and hearing. Some of the grandchildren had normal hearing and speech. I never had a chance to discuss the problem from a genetic standpoint.

The sister explained how I happened to be there. They signed back and forth, giving me surreptitious glances from time to time. I tried not to look discomfited in any way. It wasn't easy. It was the first baby and progress was slow. She was only minimally dilated. I sat around and timed her contractions for an hour or so, and then told the Sister-in-Charge that I would go back to the office and return later to check on things. The group held a signing conference, looking very doubtful that this was the proper procedure for the doctor to take. But I left.

I managed to get some lunch before they called me again. I was ordered to hurry. I did.

Contractions were still the same, she was a bit more dilated and considerably more vocal. Just because a person can't talk doesn't mean that they can't yell.

The sign conference continued during the afternoon. I don't know that they were talking about me, but they were looking at me while they were signing.

By late afternoon she was still only about 4 cms dilated and the head had not progressed any. I decided to go home for supper. I would be back later I told them. They discussed it on their fingers, all the while giving me suspicious and doubtful looks.

I managed to eat supper before they called again. Hurry, they said. I hurried. After all, it had only been a week or so since I had sworn to Apollo and Aesculapius, and probably Hippocrates by way of association, that I would do nothing but good things, and no bad things, like not hurrying.

She was about five centimeters dilated, the contractions were pretty good, but not very close together. The baby's heart rate was good, the mother was doing fine, and her vocal level had risen several decibels. The attendants were signing so fast I could almost hear their fingers move. I gave the mother-to-be a small dose of medicine for her pain. She smiled gratefully. One of the signers brought me some iced tea.

The night progressed a lot faster than the labor. Finally, about 4:00 AM, I began to get anxious. This was my first delivery unsupervised, and there weren't a bunch of nurses running around, or OB residents nearby to lean on. I was down in the trenches by myself.

I choked. I suggested that we call an ambulance and take her to the hospital. Signs flew like mad. Everybody agreed. The ambulance was called and arrived in about thirty minutes. This was back country and a dirt road.

We got her to the hospital and admitted. I was down in the waiting room writing notes to the father, telling him that it would probably be a few hours yet, that things were fine and there was nothing to worry about, and I had everything under control. (And boy did I ever hope so!) A nurse stuck her head in the door and said that I was wanted in the delivery room stat!

It was a boy, a fine healthy boy with excellent lungs and vocal cords, though it would be a while before we would know if they worked properly.

The husband was grateful. The poor lady had suffered for hours, and then this brilliant young doctor (or so I fantasized) had taken her to the hospital and ended her suffering by delivering a fine, healthy boy. I never mentioned that I thought a very light weight ambulance, bouncing over a gravel road, may have stimulated a labor that was progressing normally, to be a little more active.

The baby was named for me, and it is an honor that I have often recalled with pride. And that is why I was so proud of the child/man who was acting as my interpreter. He did a magnificent job!

≈20≋

THE TASTE TEST

I was heading back to the office after a series of house calls, and at the last house I had asked the patient to give me a urine sample to take back to the office for examination. Patients used any receptacle that was handy, a jar, a bottle, and in this case a pint whiskey bottle-brown glass and a cork stopper of a much favored, cheap brand of blended whiskey. As was usually the case, they put it in a brown paper bag, or a poke as many of the people called it in that section of the country.

I wasn't far down the road when I came to a hitch-hiker. The man was well known to all of us in the area, a hardworking, honest-as-the-day-is-long type, not real swift in the head, and he spoke with a lisp. I stopped and he crawled in the Jeep. I explained that I had one more house call before going back to town.

I made my last house call and we continued back toward town. When we reached the point where my passenger wanted to get out, I pulled off on the shoulder of the highway. He hesitated a moment and then got out and leaned back through the window; a very serious expression clouded his face. He was obviously embarrassed, and struggling hard to be diplomatic. He said, "Doc, I don't know what kind of withkey you drink, but to me it tathe justh like pith."

≈ ≋

~21~

ON COUGH MEDICINE

He was an old man, up in his eighties, and not long retired as an engineer for the Chesapeake and Ohio Railroad. In those days engineers held on for a long time, much to the distress of the firemen who were waiting for a vacancy so they could move over to the right side of the locomotive. But he had problems and had been forced to retire.

It was his heart that caused his retirement. It was also his heart that caused the chronic, dry, hacking cough that disturbed him so. No matter how hard I tried to explain what was causing his cough, he continued to blame it on a cold, bronchitis, or whatever.

During one of my visits he asked if I thought Rock and Rye, a mixture of rye whiskey and rock candy, was a good cough medicine. I agreed that it was. He wanted me to write a prescription for some. I said it didn't require a prescription. Just go to the liquor store, buy a bottle of bourbon, go to the grocery store or wherever, and buy some rock candy, pour the bourbon over the candy, and he was in business. For that matter, just sugar could replace the rock candy.

Well, that wouldn't do at all, that was like drinking a toddy. It had to be rye because rye was "medicinal," and he didn't want to go to the liquor store because somebody might see him and tell the railroad, and they took a dim view of their men drinking. The fact that he was now retired made no difference, his loyalty was still strong.

I told him I would take care of it for him, and I did. I told him to take a couple of teaspoonsful before meals and at bedtime as needed.

A week or so later I went to check on him. He was raving about his cough medicine. Best he had ever tried. Didn't cough much anymore, as long as he took his medicine, but miss one dose and it started right up again. He also said that he had increased the dose occasionally.

"And I'll tell you something else, Doc. Ever since I got that cough medicine I've had more visitors than I ever had in my life, and you know every damn one of them has got a cough and want to try out my medicine." He showed me his almost empty bottle.

"You're going to have to get me another prescription of this before the weekend."

≈ ≋

❧22❧

QUOTH THE RAVEN

"It's time for his checkup," the lady on the other end of the phone said, "and come at dinner time." Dinner time was noon. The lady was Ethel Crawford, calling about her husband, Lark. She always wanted me to come at dinner time, and I always enjoyed going at dinner time.

Mr. Crawford was almost ninety. He was one of those venerable gentlemen who had grown up with the ethic that hard work, honesty, and a strong belief in The Almighty was what made America, West Virginia, Raleigh County, and especially the Shady Spring District, strong. He had been a farmer, a timber man, and just about everything else too, I expect. His farm was beautiful, flat cropland and pasture. His cattle were sleek. His sheep were neatly sheared in summer and thick with wool in winter. Chickens pecked about the yard with complete trust, even coming to the gate to greet me as I drove up. The pet crow that sat on the high back of his chair always said "Hi Doc," as an echo to Mr. Crawford's similar greeting.

As usual, Mr. Crawford was sitting in a rocking chair in his bedroom, a coal fire burning in the grate as always, winter and summer. A thick sheepskin padded the rocking chair seat, and another, the back of the chair. Mr. Crawford had his legs drawn up in the chair with his arms locked about his knees, in a position that amazed me for a person of any age. He looked very comfortable. His blood pressure was holding well, his heart and lungs were clear. He didn't have any edema of his extremities. His shins were dry and scaling, and itched terribly. I told him to use some skin lotion on his legs, and to not sit so close to the open fire. But I told him that every time that I went to see him.

He began telling me about an old doctor who used to live in the general area, long before I could remember.

"I went down to see him about a breaking out I had on my body. Old Doc took a look at it and said, 'Lark, you got the seven year itch, and you're two weeks behind on your scratchin'.'"

And then he broke up laughing, "Heh, heh, heh . . . ."

Abner, the crow, said, "That's funny, that's funny. Haw, haw."

Abner sailed off the back of the chair and strutted over to the screened door and called out, "Heah, heah!" sounding for all the world like Mrs. Crawford. The nondescript dog that lived in the yard came bounding up on the back porch, tongue lolling happily, and tail waving rapidly in anticipation of a handout. By that time Abner was at the front door calling "Heah, heah!" The dog came running around the house and Abner strutted back to Mr. Crawford's chair and flapped his wings to lift himself to his usual perch. If his beak could bend in such a shape, he would have been smiling. Mr. Crawford began his wheezing laughter, "Heh, heh, heh . . . ." Abner said, "Haw, haw."

Mrs. Crawford stood at the doorway, shaking her head. "That bird is going to drive that poor dog out of his mind," she said.

"Abner, shame on you! Stop teasing that dog," she scolded, shaking her finger at the crow, just as she would at a child. Abner flapped his wings, and right on cue he croaked, "Nevermore, nevermore."

Mr. Crawford wheezed his laughter, "Heh, heh." Abner strutted proudly across the back of the chair. "Haw, haw," he said.

Mrs. Crawford then announced that dinner was ready.

The table was loaded with roast beef, pork chops, potatoes, green beans, stewed tomatoes, pinto beans, cabbage, cornbread, biscuits, chocolate cake and cherry pie. I ate alone. Abner sat on the edge of the table and watched, and played with a match box that contained a quarter. He liked to rattle the box and then push it open to look at the quarter. He would then shut the box and rattle it again.

On a few occasions there had been other guests who just happened to drop in. Every time I was there it was the same, the menu varying only slightly, sometimes including baked ham and/or chicken, other vegetables in the summer, and different desserts, always cake and pie, just different flavors.

After all of that, they expected to pay me for the house call. I charged them the same as it would have been for a repeat office call, $2.00. It wasn't but about a twenty-mile round trip to their house, and if they had a car, and if Mr. Crawford had been able, they would have come to the office, and just think what I would have missed.

≈ ≈

SNAKES, STICKS AND TOES

The summer turned hot very early. By June the growth was so heavy along the old railroad bed that followed Glade creek from its mouth to its source that I couldn't get my friend, Charlie Anderson, to go trout fishing there. He didn't like snakes, and Glade creek was noted for its snakes.

The young boy hopped into the examining room on one foot, carrying his sneaker in his hand. A trail of blood had followed him from the door to the table. His little toe looked like it had been put through a grinder.

"What happened to you," I asked.

"Daddy beat it with a stick," he said.

This was long before child abuse became a national pastime, so such a thought never entered my mind. The father, standing behind me, laughed.

The boy said that they had been down on Glade fishing, and he was walking down the old grade, had stepped over a log and heard a rattlesnake buzz. "I looked around, and then realized that I was standing on it, my foot just behind its head. I called for Dad, and told him what had happened. He said, 'Git off of it.' I said I couldn't cause it would bite me."

The father took over, "I came running up and saw what the situation was. I looked around and found a stick and started hitting the snake on the head."

The boy interrupted, "You mean you started hitting me on the toe. You hit me at least ten times before you ever touched the durn snake." The father laughed. "Yeah, and every time I yelled, you'd laugh and say, 'I'll get it next time,' and then you'd whomp me again. I bet it's broke." The boy was grinning. They had obviously enjoyed at least part of the tragedy.

The father had eventually hit the snake enough times to kill it, and had the rattles to prove it. Ten rattles and a button. It was a big snake.

≈24≈

TROUBLES THAT CHILDREN GET INTO

Sometime early in my practice, a salesman talked me into buying an instrument to remove foreign objects from noses and ears. It had a little flat blade that was just a couple of millimeters wide and not much longer and, when a trigger was pulled, this little flat blade flexed downward and the instrument could be withdrawn from the ear or nose, pulling the object with it. It sat around on a shelf for a couple of years.

Finally a mother rushed in with her little girl. She had a kernel of corn up her nose. We put the child on the table and I cautioned Bessie to hold her tight, with her arms up beside her head so that she couldn't turn it. The child screamed and kicked.

I took my marvelous little instrument and began pushing it past the kernel of corn, pushed the trigger, the blade flexed and it pulled the kernel right out of the nose, just like the salesman said it would, and dropped it right in the screaming child's mouth. He hadn't mentioned that possibility. Thank goodness she swallowed it rather than aspirating it into her trachea. That was the only time that I had occasion to use it. I don't think that children put things up their noses as often as the salesman indicated.

Another child came in with something in the ear. The mother said it was a candlefly, a small moth that flits around a light in summer. I had my doubts that such a fly could, or would, get in a child's ear. I got my otoscope and looked. Have you ever looked a moth in the face, under magnification, and in bright light? It's scary!

I never did figure out how that moth got there. It had to have backed in; there is no way it could crawl in and turn around, judging from the difficulty I had extracting it. I couldn't use my special instrument.

Children get into all kinds of trouble. One frantic mother rushed in with her child who was passing pure blood in her urine. She had a specimen with her. The child looked fine. Certainly she didn't appear ill enough to have gross hematuria.

The urinalysis was negative for blood and anything else. On further questioning the mother remembered that the little girl had eaten an entire jar of beets.

Another foreign body that I saw happened while I was in the Navy and was on duty one night in a Dispensary. The father rushed in saying that the child had swallowed a quarter. The boy was about three. I didn't think that there was going to be a problem, and there was no need for an X-ray.

The father was a Commander, I was a Lieutenant (j.g.), and he wanted an X-ray.

I ordered an X-ray.

I took the developed film back to the rank-happy father and informed him that the child had not swallowed a quarter.

He got all huffed up and said, "He did so, because I stood right there and watched him."

I told him it wasn't a quarter, it was a nickel, and it had come up heads, and I showed him the film. There, very plainly, could be seen the coin in the child's stomach, and the outline of a buffalo on it.

The father also didn't find much humor in the old cliché, "Call me if there is any change."

25

CROSSING THE BAR

Sunset and evening star,
And one clear call for me!
And may there be no moaning of the bar,
When I put out to sea . . . .
(Alfred, Lord Tennyson)

Mr. and Mrs. Welsh were from Scotland. They came over in the early part of the century and had lived at Raleigh for longer than I could remember. Their children had grown up there, except one who died in his early teens from meningitis. For me it was always a pleasure to see them whenever their daughter-in-law called. They lived next door to their son and his family.

Mrs. Welsh was lying in the bed, her ruddy face flushed with a slight fever, and coughing repeatedly so that her plump body shook the bed.

"I looked out the window two days ago and there she stood, hanging up sheets, and you know how cold its been this week," Violet said. "I really fussed at her about that. She already had a slight cold anyway."

Mrs. Welsh's clear blue eyes flashed in indignation, and in her rich Scots' voice said, "I juust toold hir, tha wus I ganna dee, I wus ganna dee betwin clean sheets."

Her husband was Tom. He was as gaunt as she was ample. His pale blue eyes were surrounded by a wrinkled squint, as if they had never become accustomed to the daylight, after long years in the darkness of a coal mine. He sat most of the time in a rocking chair by a window and kept company with his memories. In the summer he and his chair and his memories would rock on the porch.

He was sitting in his chair when I arrived in response to the call. His eyes were closed. His hands were resting as always on the arms of the rocker. He looked very normal except that he was dead. Just like that; no sound, no suffering, just passed from life as we know it, to a life that someday we will know. To me that has always seemed a good way to cross over the bar. However, it was now my duty to tell Mrs. Welsh in the next room.

"Mrs. Welsh," I said, "Mr. Welsh has, has, uh, passed away." She sat for a moment without speaking. I was certain that she must have suspected something from the way I had rushed in without stopping to speak with her. Finally she shook her head, sadly, "Pur auld Tom, and I juust bought 'im a new switer yisterday," she said, tears seeping from between closed lids, from eyes that were no doubt replaying scenes of days past; days of moors and heather, days of youth and love, days that only she was left to remember.

≈ ≈

26

MISS AMERICA

It always seemed strange to me that a child would be given the name America. For this particular woman I think it may have had something to do with the date of her birth, July 4, 1876. I always called her Miss America. The Miss out of deference to her age, and combined with her name because I liked the sound of it. Of course she came long before the Miss America Pageant had ever been considered, but if there had been such an event, and she was of the age of participation in such activities, and so inclined, she would have been qualified in all respects, and I am certain that she would have at least ended up as Miss Congeniality.

I had seen her on several occasions for colds, bronchitis and other minor ailments, but it had been well over a year when she appeared in the office again. She was complaining of a lump that she noticed for several months, and it seemed to be getting larger. It was in her breast.

The lump was easily palpable. Also the skin over the lump was pitted, the classical orange peel sign of inflammatory adenocarcinoma of the breast. This is a cancerous inflammation that has invaded the lymphatic system of the breast and is an ominous sign.

I sent her to a surgeon and a radical mastectomy was done. Not enough skin was left to completely cover the defect, as was usually the case, and a skin graft was applied. Some of that didn't take and it required changes of dressings.

Miss America lived on the side of a mountain laced with laurel thickets that surrounded grown up fields, and an orchard of apple trees that had been in their prime when Miss America celebrated the Fourth for her first time.

I would go out and change her dressings and check on her progress once a week. A young girl that stayed with her would care for the wound, very capably, the rest of the time.

On this particular day it was late in the afternoon that I arrived at her house, accompanied by Sally, my English pointer. I checked the wound and it looked great. Where the graft had failed, some granulation tissue was forming. I touched the margins of the wound with some Scarlet Red ointment to stimulate granulation and reapplied the dressing. Then Sally and I headed for the mountainside and the old orchard.

Hunting was pretty good. Sally worked well, pointed several grouse and, if my shooting had been as good as her pointing, it would have been a super day.

It was getting late, and dark comes early in the mountains, so when we got back to the yard through which we would have to pass to get to the car, Miss America's chickens were trying to find comfortable roosting spots. One agitated hen squawked, and flapped her wings, and ran right under Sally's nose. She grabbed it and, the harder the hen struggled, the harder Sally clamped down. She had never been an ideal retriever anyhow, and I frequently had to almost fight her for a bird, but she had never before killed a chicken.

I got it away from her and put her in the car. Then I took the remains of the Plymouth Rock egg layer up to the house. Miss America said not to worry about it, she had a hankering for chicken and dumplings anyway.

The young girl that stayed with Miss America didn't look too happy about the chore that she felt would soon be hers, so I said I would dress the chicken if she would bring me a some hot water out to the back of the house.

I don't think that I put enough emphasis on the word hot. Even though the bucket of water was steaming, I forgot that, when the outside temperature is in the thirties, even lukewarm water will steam. I realized it soon enough when I immersed the chicken and found that the body of the chicken was warmer than the water, but by then the damage had been done, and little Miss Caretaker had disappeared back to the warmth of her kitchen.

Picking a cold, wet chicken is not easy. Feathers stuck to my hands, caught on my clothes, and swirled about my face. Other feathers were pushed deep into the flesh of the chicken where Sally's tooth marks were. I doubt that Sally ever knew just how close she came to becoming a casualty herself.

I finally got the job done and presented the carcass to a much relieved young girl. Miss America thought I had done way too much and that I should take the chicken home with me but I declined. After my recent experience I had no desire for chicken at all, in any form.

But Sally did. She never got over the event and I had to be extremely careful about where I hunted. Just a week later, while quail hunting, I lost her. She didn't respond to my whistle or calls. I backtracked to the house where we had started and there she was, digging like mad to get under the door of a chicken house in which the farmer had luckily fastened his chickens before he left for town.

I saw Miss America frequently over the next several months for various medical complaints. She was always the same cheerful person, speaking in a soft, melodious voice. Even when she became hoarse and complained that she always had the feeling that she had to clear her throat, there remained the same soft smile that played about her lips as she talked.

X-rays showed enlarged lymph nodes in her mediastinum, the middle of her chest. The lymph nodes, filled with cancer, had involved a nerve to the vocal cord, the recurrent laryngeal nerve, along with a lot of other structures.

She went off to receive radiation treatments and never returned.

≈ ≋

≈27≈

FIRE AND PAIN AND FEAR

Mr. W. was very tall, and so thin that if he turned sideways he would scarcely cast a shadow. His Adam's apple stuck out like a coat hook and rode up and down over his collar as he talked in a deep, slightly hoarse voice. He was always dressed in a shirt and tie, and a rusty black suit coat that he wore over his bib overalls. I never knew how old he was because he was never a patient. His visits to my office were always on behalf of his wife. But I knew he was old; he had appeared old when I was a child and we had hunted at his farm. He appeared just as old now, but age is relative to the beholder. They had sold the farm for what may have seemed like a good price, but was probably much less than its actual worth, and were now living in a small house closer to civilization but still primitive, without water and electricity. The circumstances of his life had not left him without dignity.

He would walk into my office and take a seat beside the desk and cross his legs. His legs crossed so high that it looked as if he was crossing his hips. Then he would clear his throat and begin his speech by saying, "Well sir . . . ." Every paragraph that he spoke began that way. Generally it was a request for some type of medicine for "The Missus," as he referred to her. Most often he gave a long review of her symptoms, followed by a synopsis of her past history, and what he thought should be the treatment. Most of the time we were in complete agreement as to the therapy. Sometimes, however, I would feel that perhaps I had better go to see her. This was almost always the case in winter because he had usually walked the three miles or so from his house to the office. I would tell him to wait and I would drive him home. He would then get up out of the chair, and it always reminded me of the unfolding of a carpenter's rule as he uncrossed his legs and multiple joints would begin to straighten as he assumed the erect position. He would again clear his throat and say, "Well sir, if you feel it is absolutely necessary, I'll be just outside in the waiting room."

Mrs. W. was pitiful. She was little and thin, but the most devastating thing about her appearance was her face. Many years ago, how long I never knew, she had been cooking a meal, had a convulsive seizure and had fallen face down on the stove. Most of her nose was missing, and burn scars contracted her mouth and her eyelids of one eye, making the other eye appear abnormally large. Her hands and forearms had also suffered severe burns, and for the most part her hands were useless for any but the most basic of activities.

At one time, somebody had put her on Phenobarbital, probably for control of her seizures. If she ever had another seizure I never knew of it, but I kept her on the Phenobarbital just in case.

Some of the time she was ill with upper respiratory infections, a GI complaint, a urinary tract infection, or something treatable. Most of the time her medical problems were so illusory, so incomprehensible, it was difficult to sit and listen. But, one look at her and at her surroundings compelled my attention. It was always pain that she complained about in a high, whining, monotonic voice.

"The pain begins here," she would say, pointing to the side of her head, the most scarred side, "and runs right down this side into my foot, and then it jumps across into the other foot and back up that leg and when it gets to my head again, it just almost kills me."

In the meantime her husband had folded up his carpenter-rule body into a straight chair beside the table in their dining room/living room/bedroom, crossed his legs at the hips again, and was nodding in agreement. "Well sir, she actually screamed with pain, it was so bad last night," he would say.

I could never find anything that I could actually treat. It always seemed that sitting and listening, nodding in agreement with the two of them, would give enough encouragement for her to face a few more days of life, such as it was. Most of her attacks of pain happened at night and I have often wondered if it was a recurrent dream of fire and hot stoves and being unable to move.

Mr. W. would reach for his purse as I was leaving. I would tell him that I would send it into the "Office," as he always referred to the Department of Public Assistance. "Well sir, if they don't pay, you let me know and I'll make it good."

≈ ≈

≈28≈

POLIO AND A TOUCH OF CLASS

The summer I arrived was a bad year for polio. It had been bad most everywhere that year. Numerous children presented with fever, headache, runny noses, joint pains, and stomach complaints. Parents were frantic with any symptom. Some of the children did have poliomyelitis, except most everybody called it infantile paralysis.

One case was at White Oak. I sent the child to Milton where a Children's Hospital was located and was the center for treatment of the disease. She was gone for several weeks and returned home with a weak leg but no other residuals and did very well.

Another child began with a high fever, followed by a convulsion. Because of some rigidity of her neck, I had her taken to the hospital where a spinal tap showed the classical findings of polio. She was still having some muscular twitchings and I was afraid that perhaps she was developing the bulbar type of the disease, the kind that might require the use of an "iron lung." In order to get her to Milton, we called an ambulance, and borrowed a portable iron lung from the Fire Department.

We got the child loaded up and I crawled in the back beside her. I told the driver that speed and sirens were not necessary, just get us to Milton about one hundred miles west. The family would follow in their car.

The ambulances at that time were furnished by funeral homes. They were comfortable. The drivers were generally young men, some perhaps with aspirations of becoming Funeral Directors, and all of them with aspirations to become race car drivers, and maybe even qualify for the Indianapolis 500. They liked to practice their driving skills in the ambulance.

Our driver was very sensible until he approached the toll booth at the newly completed West Virginia Turnpike. He called out to the toll taker to notify Charleston that we were coming and to have a police escort at the western end of the turnpike, and we were off to the races.

With the siren screaming and lights flashing, we tore down the road. It was two lanes then, and considered by many as the most dangerous turnpike, if not the most dangerous road, in America. I kept trying to get his attention to slow him down, but I was afraid to divert his attention too much, or he might try to look back at me.

The Charleston police had a motorcycle escort at the Charleston exit. He took off like a relay runner, looking back and waving to our driver to hurry up. He was a good fifty yards ahead of us as we went down Kanawha Boulevard. At the intersection of Boulevard and Capitol street, I could see the traffic piled up. The policeman stood up on the pedals of his Harley and motioned with both hands over his head for the traffic to open up. There was a slight dip in the street at that intersection. The motorcycle went airborne for about fifty feet. I shut my eyes. Then the ambulance went airborne and when it came down I went airborne right to the roof of the vehicle.

South Charleston went by so quickly that there was no smell. The rest of the trip was a piece of cake, and Milton was beautiful to behold. I was alive and well and thankful.

We got the child admitted. She had made the trip without incident and fortunately had no further problems. There was some temporary paralysis but no permanent residuals. The parents had not arrived but my driver was anxious to get back home, so we had to leave. We passed the family about St. Albans. They were almost an hour behind us and the father told me later that he had driven fast. (That's what he thought.)

We were going up the turnpike, approaching the tunnel, when a siren sounded behind us. A state trooper pulled us over. He said, "I watched you going down with that patient. You don't have any excuse on the way home." He handed out the ticket so fast that I think he must have written it out ahead of time in anticipation.

The Salk vaccine came along in 1955 and the polio problem abated, and eventually ended.

I was awakened one night by a call from a woman saying something about a sick child. Then I awoke and found the telephone lying across my chest. The dial tone was buzzing loudly. I could recall a woman's voice and something about a sick child, but I didn't have the foggiest idea of who had called, or how long it had been. I put the phone in the cradle and it rang almost immediately.

"Doc, you fell asleep while I was talking to you," the woman said. "I could hear you snoring. Are you awake now?"

I assured her I was.

She identified herself, and said that she thought her daughter had polio. Everything began coming together for me, the name, the disease, and the address. I said, "She's had polio, she's had the Salk vaccine. She can't have polio."

"Doc, you get out of bed and come out here. I say she's got the polio." The voice was strident and insistent. I dared not resist any longer.

I drove out to White Oak with my trousers pulled on over my pajamas, and a corduroy jacket over a T shirt. I was wearing my bedroom slippers.

The child had all of the symptoms and findings of polio, and it was confirmed by spinal tap. She spent a few weeks at Milton again, and returned home with no residuals.

The mother had real class. She never once said, "I told you so."

CHILDHOOD DISEASES:
YOU NEVER FORGET THE SOUND OF A WHOOP

Childhood diseases, for the most part, were not serious. There were the usual cases of measles, roseola, and from time to time there were cases of scarlatina. Mumps came in waves.

In a number of diseases, immunity can be transferred from the mother to the baby across the placenta. This is not true of pertussis, or whooping cough as it is commonly known.

Even though immunization had been around for whooping cough for a long time, there were still sporadic cases of it because parents didn't think it was important enough. I think there are still parents who feel that way, who feel that it won't happen to their child . . . the "no one ever has that any more" attitude. Some politicians think it is due to the cost. It isn't that. Many who complain about the cost still find the money to buy a couple of six packs of beer and cartons of cigarettes. The real reason that children don't get their immunizations is NEGLECT.

The immunizations are available at County Health Clinics for those without family physicians, and are free or at a nominal cost. Years ago it was the same. Anyone who has seen and heard a baby with whooping cough will never forget that an immunization could have prevented it.

The baby was five months old. A husky baby, but listless from the fatigue of the paroxysms of coughing that ended in the high pitched inhalation that was the characteristic whoop from which the disease got its name. The mother was almost as listless; her pinched face was pale and dark circles framed eyes that were dull with fatigue. She had been holding the baby for 24 hours.

The mother was sitting on the porch with her baby, hoping that the fresh summer morning air might help the baby breathe. When she had called, she said the baby had bronchitis and had been sick for about a week and was getting worse. A paroxysm had begun as I walked up the path from the road, and the whoop occurred as I mounted the steps. The baby's head was limp on the mother's arm when I reached the porch. She and the baby both smelled of sour milk from the vomiting of every bottle that the child had tried to take for the past two days.

The tiny eyes were half shut; when I pushed open an eyelid, the sclera, the white part of the eye, was covered by a dense hemorrhage underneath the outer covering, the conjunctiva. Small blood vessels had ruptured from the force of the coughing.

Another paroxysm was beginning, first slowly, then building up more rapidly, harder, harsher, the child's face changing from red to purple to a dusky blue, and finally the crescendo, the whoop. Once again the little head dropped loosely onto the mother's arm. She wiped at the stringy mucous hanging from the baby's mouth with a diaper that smelled of sour milk, and finally used her fingers to pull the four or five inch strand of thick, yellow mucous out of the mouth.

The child needed fluids. The child needed care that could not be given at home. I went to a neighbor's house and called a pediatrician friend. Could we get this child in the hospital? He would try; he would arrange for isolation; bring it on in.

The father came home from work, and he and the mother drove the fifteen miles to the hospital.

A paroxysm began just minutes away from the hospital but there was no whoop at the end. A plug of mucous prevented the whoop. It also prevented a life-saving breath. The dusky blue head flopped over on the mother's arm for the last time.

A simple immunization could have prevented it.

I had never had mumps and I was always uneasy when I saw a child with the disease, but I continued to treat them. There was little to do except go and look, give the parents some moral support, and try not to get too close.

One child however was quite ill. She was about eight years old. She had fever and vomiting. Eventually she complained of headache and I became very concerned. I went back one evening, having been there earlier in the day. I had decided that if she didn't improve that I was going to get some help on this case. Her fever was down, her headache was better, and she had an engaging smile that was comforting to see, even though her face was still puffed up like a greedy chipmunk. It told me that things were better.

The father walked out to the Jeep with me. You know, when a family member does that, there is something to be discussed.

"You thought she had encephalitis, didn't you Doctor," he said.

I acknowledged that I had been worried about that, and I did expect that she had had a mild form of it.

He said, "I thought so too. You know, our first daughter died with encephalitis when she had mumps. She was just this age."

Years later, when I was the Orthopaedic Resident at Cripple Children's Hospital in Richmond, I finally succumbed to mumps when case after case swept through the hospital. I too had fever, and vomiting, and a headache that made my head feel as if it would explode. I woke up the morning before Christmas and knew that it had finally caught up with me.

We celebrated Christmas immediately because I suspected that I would not feel very well the next day. One of my children gave me a highly advertised after-shave lotion, which I dutifully used that day.

True to my expectations, Christmas Day found me prostrate with a high fever and a severe headache, and nausea and vomiting. The scent of the after-shave held on tenaciously, and I haven't been able to tolerate the smell of any after-shave since that time. That was my only residual of the disease.

≈ ⊱

≈30≈

I AM CONVINCED THAT HYPNOSIS IS FOR REAL

A dentist friend who was interested in hypnosis was discussing it in a general conversation one evening and sensed my cynical, if not completely negative, attitude, that it could be used for any practical purpose. He suggested that it could even be used for obstetrics.

In order to convince me that hypnosis was a valid entity and not just a bunch of mumbo jumbo, he hypnotized me and made me a believer. That was when I started thinking about trying it in obstetrics.

There was a lady who was pregnant who I thought would be an ideal test of this. She was willing to try it. I told my father about it, he having delivered her and known her all of her life, as well all the rest of the family. He laughed. He said it would never work on her.

It took some training. She went to my friend's office several times for these sessions. Finally one day he called to tell me that, as a test, he had given her a post-hypnotic suggestion that she would call me on the phone on a certain day, at a certain time.

On the appointed day, at the appointed time, the phone rang. It was my patient. She chatted about the weather and some other vague stuff, and I asked her why she had called, was everything okay. She hesitated for a moment and then answered that she didn't know why she had called, she was washing dishes, had looked up at the clock and called me. She apologized for bothering me. I then explained to her what had happened. She was excited to know that this business of hypnosis was really working. She also had been rather cynical in her beliefs, I found out later. We decided to go on with the experiment.

Her expected date for delivery seemed to be right on target, considering all factors. The head was already engaged and the cervix was effaced. My colleague even gave her a post hypnotic suggestion that she would begin contractions at a certain time. I had become enough of a believer that I made sure he didn't get me involved in the middle of the night. Sure enough, the contractions began in the late afternoon.

We all met at the hospital and labor progressed normally, and fairly rapidly, over the course of two or three hours. She never complained of pain or discomfort. The baby never seemed stressed. It was a nice labor.

When dilatation was complete, we moved into the delivery room. Ed gave her some reinforcement, I guess it could be called, and the baby was delivered without any problem. She had a slight perineal tear which I sutured without using any xylocaine. She denied having any pain or discomfort during the entire process.

I guess it worked. Knowing her, it must have. The baby is proof of that.

I never had a chance to try it on others. Shortly after that I left for Richmond to take a residency in Orthopaedic Surgery and left General Practice behind.

CUTTING THE TIES THAT BIND

It seemed that the village of Beaver had difficulty in keeping their doctors. The doctor that preceded me left after six years to take a residency in Ear, Nose and Throat. A good friend of mine with whom I had worked closely left his practice in Beckley to take a residency in Obstetrics. Now, after six years of a country practice, I decided to leave for a residency in Orthopaedic Surgery at the Veterans Administration Hospital in Richmond, Virginia. It was no reflection on Beaver or on the patients that I had cared for, and that I cared about very much. It was just time to move on.

When I had left the Navy in 1952 I had plans of someday taking a residency but decided instead to try general practice first. I am glad that I did. It gave me a philosophy of medicine that is not taught anywhere in books, and certainly not in medical school.

It was a difficult transition to make from treating "the skin and its contents" (as general practice was frequently referred to) to limiting yourself to one field. That fact was pointed out to me very quickly.

I had been a Junior Resident for about a month when an old man with a broken hip went into acute cardiac failure following his hip nailing. He had developed a supraventricular tachycardia, a very rapid heart rate due to something triggering the electrical impulses from the heart's control center. The fear showing on his face was striking. I digitalized him using Digitoxin, an alkaloid of digitalis, and his heart rate slowed, his respirations improved, his urinary output increased, and, best of all, the expression of impending disaster on his face disappeared. That is almost a sure sign that a patient with acute heart failure is improved.

At rounds the next morning the Chief of the service remarked on the man's improvement and I told him that I had digitalized him during the night. He asked who had done the medical consult and I told him that I had not gotten one. He gently let me know that I was now a surgeon, and things medical should be left to Internal Medicine.

By Christmas I was well adjusted to the changes that Orthopaedic Surgery had enforced on me, but I had not quite hardened myself to ignoring certain obvious signs.

I was making rounds on Christmas morning, a lonely time on a hospital ward. It was quiet; it was dim and melancholy. Each patient said "Merry Christmas"; I am sure they meant it for me but didn't feel it for themselves.

I went back to the Nurse's Station and wrote an order in the chart of each of the forty-seven patients for two ounces of bourbon before dinner and before supper for those that desired it, and one ounce as a "nightcap" if desired. Practically everybody took their ration, and if they didn't I am sure that a couple of the orderlies managed to dispose of it.

Dinner was at 12:30, the typical Christmas dinner of turkey and all the trimmings, with ice cream in the shape of little Santa Clauses for dessert. I went back to the ward later in the afternoon to find the lights on and the patients laughing and singing. One of the Volunteers had rolled a piano up to the ward and a visitor had joined in the merriment by playing Christmas Carols and other Christmas songs.

By late evening some of the music was more suitable for a barracks than a hospital ward.

The next day my boss came into my office with an amused expression on his face. "Do you want to explain what went on up here yesterday?" he asked.

I told him how depressed everybody had been, and I didn't see why they couldn't have a bit of "Christmas Cheer," so I had ordered drinks all around for those who wanted it before dinner, supper, and at bedtime.

He then told me that the Chief of Pharmacy had called the Director of the Hospital, who in turn called the Chief of Surgery, who in turn called the Chief of Orthopaedics. Both the Chief of Surgery and my chief had defended my action.

My chief said, "I don't think anybody else ever had the guts to do it. You really cleaned out the Pharmacy's liquor cabinet though. It put a helluva hole in the Pharmacy's budget too."

I strayed out of my bounds another time too when we had an old man, a Spanish-American War veteran from the foothills of the Blue Ridge, admitted with a fractured hip. He was accompanied by his two daughters, not only because of their concern but also to speak for him because he was deaf.

"You have to yell in his ear for him to hear anything at all, Doctor," one of his daughters told me. "He's been deaf for at least ten years."

"More like twenty years," the other daughter added.

So, as instructed, I leaned over and yelled in his ear about what he had and what we were going to do about it. He may have heard some of it, but at least the daughters heard that he would have his hip operated on the next morning at 0800. They were satisfied and left to spend the night with a cousin in nearby Chesterfield County.

We got the old gentleman settled, and in the course of my examination I found that his poor old deaf ears were packed with dense, hard wax. Since he didn't seem too uncomfortable with his injury, I had the nurse put some oil in his ears to soften the wax and then syringed them, washing out the plugs of wax. The man's eyes brightened up with amazement at all the things he could hear.

The next morning he went to surgery and the operation went quickly. After recovering from the anesthesia, but still a bit groggy, he was brought back to the ward where his daughters were waiting with filial devotion.

Daddy was lying in his bed in peaceful repose when one of his daughters leaned over, her lips nearly touching his ear, and said, "Daddy, it's Mary Alice. CAN YOU HEAR ME?"

Daddy almost jumped out of bed. In startled, wild-eyed fury, he grabbed his traumatized ear and shouted, "GOL DARN IT, OF COURSE I CAN HEAR YOU. YOU THINK I'M DEAF OR SOMETHING?"

The four years of residency passed quickly, the final year being spent at Crippled Children's Hospital in Richmond where I managed to contract mumps while playing kind, friendly, pediatrician in addition to orthopaedic surgeon.

It is amazing to me that these children, who suffer from horrible, deforming problems that require multiple surgical procedures, can look at their surgeon with complete trust in their eyes on the day of surgery, and afterwards. Especially afterwards!

I have always wondered if there is something special in the development of the personality of a child with a congenital deformity that gives them a different philosophy of life. It seems to remain with them forever.

Residency was over and now it was back into the real world for another entirely new life. But my philosophy of medicine remained unchanged.

≈32≈

IT'S NOT HOW YOU WEAR YOUR STETHOSCOPE
THAT COUNTS

Even today, nearly forty years later, I find it hard to let go; I still sometimes stop at a patient's house and check on the progress of a back ailment or other problem.

I really feel sorry for the young people going into medicine today. It has become so complicated, so scientific, so non-personal. House calls are a relic of a past society, something that today's doctors are not likely to experience. Will they ever see a talking crow sitting on the back of the patient's chair, laughing at the same jokes? Will they ever wonder what "quilling" means? Will they ever suffer under the scrutinizing eye of a "Granny"? Will they ever feel a child pulling them into a room of a mountain cabin to show them the prettiest Christmas Tree of their life?

On the other hand, I pray that they will never see the flaccid paralysis of arms and legs that remains after a bout with poliomyelitis, or hear the crescendo of a whoop.

And I don't really care if they hang their stethoscopes about their neck like a scarf, or carry them just so in their pockets, as long as they treat each patient with dignity, regardless of that patient's status as to cleanliness, the ability to pay, or the work he pursues.

Around 2400 years ago, Hippocrates called medicine "the greatest of the Arts." At the beginning of the 20th century Sir William Osler and the other stalwarts of medicine likewise stressed their reference to the Art of Medicine.

I define the art of medicine as the ability to make a patient feel that your only concern is that patient's welfare, regardless of that patient's status in life.

A friend recently told me that his doctor never touched him. The nurse checked his blood pressure, pulse, respiration and weight. The doctor came in and listened to his heart with his stethoscope, went over his medications, maybe wrote another prescription, gave him a slip that said when to come back, and said good-bye. He didn't even shake hands, coming or going.

"I wish, just once, he would pat me on the shoulder and say how nice it was to see me, and maybe ask about my wife, or what I had been doing. I can remember when I was a child; the doctor would come to the house to see me or my sister when we were sick. He always talked with my mother and father first about stuff that had nothing to do with sickness. He always rubbed me on the head, and smiled and winked at me as he left, and I knew that I was going to get well no matter how sick I was. I would feel a lot better if my doctor today would just pat me on the shoulder when he left the room."

Hippocrates wrote, ". . . Some patients, though conscious that their condition is perilous, recover their health simply through their contentment with the goodness of the physician."

My friend has a point.

It has been a good life, being a doctor. I still see a few patients, and I find myself slipping back into giving advice about things other than my specialty. While Orthopaedic Surgery was more confining than General Practice, it did have its moments, though I seldom had the same type of contact with the patient's family as I did in General Practice.

Physicians really should consider themselves lucky to see patients, if they were all like an elderly lady with a broken hip that I admitted to the hospital. She was over ninety years of age and as bright as a wren on a summer morning, despite her pain. I asked who her family doctor was and she answered, "I ain't seen a doctor since my first baby was born. I always figgered when you had your stove going good, you shouldn't be a-foolin' with the damper."

≈ ≈

↔ EPILOGUE ↔

Many years after I left general practice, I received a letter from Mrs. Lawrence Blake. She asked if I remembered coming to see a newborn baby one New Years Day, and if I did, would I please write out a statement to that effect so that the young man could get a birth certificate to go into the service. It seemed that I had forgotten to fill out the form to send to the Health Department. Of course I remembered. Who would ever forget that little baby, with a shoestring tied in a bow about the stump of an umbilical cord?

↔ ↔